1971 INTERCOLLEGIATE ALL CANADA FOOTBALL TEAM

The End Comes Quick

LESSONS LIVE ON

Compiled and Edited by **Keith Johnston**

Foreword by **Frank Cosentino**

Copyright © 2017 by Keith Johnston

ALL RIGHTS RESERVED. No part of this book may be used or reproduced in any manner whatsoever without written permission except in the case of brief quotations embodied in critical articles or reviews.

ISBN: 978-1-7750008-0-8

Printed in the United States of America

Book Editing by Finesse Writing and Editing LLC
Cover Photo by Joe Pier
Book Cover Design by Jeanly Fresh Zamora
Book Interior by Shanmugapriya Balasubramanian

*Dedicated to the Memory of
Rick Chevers, Dave Kates, & Jeannot
Rodrigue*

THE END COMES QUICK

Success Is No Accident

"When I look back on my football days, I think of the adage: the older we get the better we were."
— *Wayne Dunkley, The University of Toronto*

"My life experiences were highly impacted by my football experience. Certainly the strong correlation between hard work and success, overcoming adversity, the need for collaboration, understanding your role and those of your teammates, mutual respect etc."
— *Bruce MacRae, University of Western Ontario*

"It is not fair to compare players from the past to players of today. Today's players are bigger and faster and the game is different."
— *Larry Smith, Bishop's University*

"My coach took me under his wing, guided me along and gave me lots of encouragement."
— *Denny Hrycaiko, University of Manitoba*

"As a salesman, as in football, you have to keep going back and trying something different until you succeed. You make another offer or renegotiate the deal. You also learn from football not to get intimidated."
— *Mel Smith, University of Alberta*

"Football turns you into a person that people can depend on because to be successful your teammates need to depend on you."
— *Brian Gervais, Dalhousie University*

"It's the people you meet, and it's those special moments when you overcome adversity as a team; when you come together as a team."
— *John Buda, University of Waterloo*

"We had a lot of good players and we had a lot of good times together. We had fun. We didn't have a lot of stars. We played as a team. No one was better than anyone else."

— *Ole Hensrud, The University of Manitoba*

"The values I learned from my coaches are character, teamwork and purpose. My values have guided me through life and I am very thankful for that."

— *Cam Innes, University of Windsor & Queens University*

"Success is the result of teamwork and collaboration. Teamwork grows when there is trust; and trust is developed in the day-to-day interactions on the practice field."

— *Keith Johnston, McMaster University*

"If you do not have passion for what you do, you will never succeed. If you haven't lost, you don't know how to win."

— *Wayne Conrad, The University of Calgary*

"Once you get out of football, if you get down and out, you bounce right back up and go at it again."

— *Dan Dulmage, University of Western Ontario*

"Most of us just can't remember much about our playing days, except for the fact that we are friends and these are moments we cherish, everything else is hard to recall. Football is the vehicle to develop friendships."

— *Paul Kilger, University of Ottawa*

"No team can be successful because of one person, it can't happen."

— *John Danaher, University of New Brunswick*

"What you learn from football is: 'the more you give, the more you get.'"

— *Max Abraham, University of Saskatchewan*

"Football has been intertwined in my whole life since I was thirteen years old. Most importantly it also helped me find my best friend and wife of 45 years, Diane"

— *George Hill, University of Western Ontario*

"The most influential part of my life has been my interaction with former players."
— *Gill Bramwell, University of Manitoba*

"It was just the camaraderie of the guys that I valued most. It was a good group of guys who hung together and became life long friends."
— *Bob Eccles, Carleton University*

"The lessons I took into life from my football career: a) Life will knock you down but you can always get back up, b) Surround yourself with good/positive people, c) Lead by example, d) Know your job."
— *Glenn Ponomarenko, University of Saskatchewan*

"Football teaches us how to have a 'Can Do' Attitude, as well as humility."
— *Bob Mincarelli, St. Francis Xavier University*

"Football taught me that I could do what it takes to get something done."
— *Chris Harber, Carleton University*

FOREWORD

Coaching People, Vanier Cup, and All-Canadians: A personal recollection

I've had a long connection with sports of all kinds. Being born into an immigrant family, my choice of sports was based on the least amount of equipment I had to buy; It was probably a pair of sneakers. They were inexpensive high-top black and whites but provided my entrance to racing contests at picnics and playgrounds. Baseball, football, and basketball quickly joined the list, both in the community and at school. Eventually, my competitive sports world was narrowed to football. High school, university, and the CFL were part of my career. Indeed, they helped to shape my outlook. I was the recipient of each coach's philosophy and approach. I was free to pick and choose the traits I would emulate and those I would overlook.

Whenever anyone asks me "what" I coached, my answer is "people." In its simplest sense, I used the sport to help each person become a better one for having come in contact with the instrument (i.e., football). I like to think that I, along with my staff, knew our Xs and Os. We developed schemes and tactics, armed our players with the means to overcome the obstacles they would meet on the football field, hopefully helped them realize that they could transfer those abilities to life away from field, and believed that we could create an environment wherein they could thrive and display their talents and grow as athletes and as people.

I read somewhere that someone said that football was the best taught subject in schools. It's easy to agree with that. There are many facets of life that are present in sports, but especially in football. There

FOREWORD

are goals, obstacles initially perceived as stumbling blocks that occasionally morph into stepping stones, and there's also a need for discipline and persistence, as well as a sense of teamwork—all challenges for the student-athlete.

In that environment, we identified that our aims would be to treat each individual as a person, student, and an athlete (in that order). Of course, we wanted to win all of our games, but everything had to be accomplished under that umbrella of importance advertised for all to see in our playbook. The onus was on us as coaches, but at the same time, the student-athlete had to organize his life so that his assignments would not be used as an excuse to avoid practice.

The national championship, known first as the College Bowl and later the Vanier Cup, was an invitational event for the first two years, 1965 and 1966. In 1967, the Vanier Cup, named after Canada's Governor-General Georges Vanier, was the official trophy of the Canadian Intercollegiate Athletic Union (CIAU). The competing teams would emerge from semi-final games in the Maritimes and Western Canada.

In 1971, the All-Canadian team of Intercollegiate All-Stars was born. Three players from our team, the 1971 Vanier Cup champion University of Western Ontario Mustangs, were selected. They were George Hill, Middle Linebacker and Captain; Bruce MacRae, Fullback; and Dan Dulmage, Defensive Lineman. All three were outstanding athletes. They worked hard, were task-oriented and determined leaders on the field, and led by example.

The same could be said of their post graduation days (as it also could be said of the great majority of our team). George Hill went on to become a success in the insurance field; Bruce MacRae made his mark as a top financial advisor, and Dan Dulmage had a successful dentistry practice and went on to play with the Hamilton Tiger-Cats in the Canadian Football League. I'm certain that every coach in the CIS today would make the same claims about their student-athletes and the All-Canadian selections as I'm doing. These are superb representatives of an outstanding group of players of the 1971 team, a group who still interacts with each other on a regular basis and who, in 2016, gathered once more in London on the 45th anniversary of the 1971 Vanier Cup Championship. Special people brought together by a special bond—All-Stars every one of them.

— *Frank Cosentino, Head Football Coach*
University of Western Ontario, 1971

PREFACE

- ✓ I refer to football as a lifetime sport: you play it when you're young and watch it when you're old.
- ✓ The number of years playing football is usually counted in single digits, perhaps even on one hand.
- ✓ Most players don't recognize the briefness of their football careers.
  - If they did, they would approach them with much more urgency.
  - Players lack this and don't fully optimize the opportunity.
  - They think there will always be another day to play and compete.
  - The end of their career approaches much too fast and often catches them by surprise.
- ✓ Almost unexpectedly, they experience:
  - the last game or playoff game as a senior in high school or college.
  - the end of their career in a playoff game, often with a loss.
  - the unfortunate reality of not making it at the next level.
- ✓ The end of a football career is often traumatic.
  - Long standing team-school affiliations cease.
  - Strong friendships end in separation.
  - "Battle" bonds that run deep are broken.
  - Careers end with a dramatic playoff loss.
  - And many careers end with a failed attempt to make it at the next level.
- ✓ To make it all the more challenging, **the end comes too quickly**, sometimes by the surprise of:
  - the last whistle,

- a tough career-ending injury,
- being cut from the team,
- no longer having "the next game."

✓ Reality sets in when what you thought you'd never miss, over time, you crave, like:

- training camp,
- double sessions,
- conditioning,
- being screamed at,
- being challenged over and over again,
- and competing.

✓ So…recognize the reality of the brevity of a football career and approach it with the highest sense of urgency possible!

- Work hard.
- Challenge yourself to do your best.
- Enjoy every day out there.
- Bond with teammates.
- Make the most of your abilities.

✓ In the end, you'll walk away fully satisfied with a result to share with your children and grandchildren.

✓ The lesson is simple:

- Train, compete, and play every day with a strong sense of urgency because **the end comes quick**.

—*Bob Mincarelli*
— *St. Francis Xavier*

Table of Contents

1971 All-Canadian Team

OFFENSE	DEFENSE
QB – Wayne Dunkley, Toronto	DE – Dan Dulmage, Western
FB – Bruce MacRae, Western	DT – Paul Kilger, Ottawa
HB – Larry Smith, Bishop's	DT – John Danaher, New Brunswick
HB – Dennis Hrycaiko, Manitoba	DE – Max Abraham, Saskatchewan
FLK – Mel Smith, Alberta	LB – George Hill, Western
OE – Jeannot Rodrigue, Ottawa	LB – Gill Bramwell, Manitoba
OE – Brian Gervais, Dalhousie	LB – Bob Eccles, Carleton
OT – John Buda, Waterloo	LB – Glenn Ponomarenko, Saskatchewan
OG – Ole Hensrud, Manitoba	DB – Bob Mincarelli, St. Francis Xavier
C – Cam Innes, Windsor	DB – Rick Chevers, Waterloo
OG – Keith Johnston, McMaster	DB – Chris Harber, Carleton
OT – Wayne Conrad, Calgary	DB – Dave Kates, Alberta

THE END COMES QUICK

Table of Contents

Success Is No Accident v
FOREWORD ix
PREFACE xi

Introduction 1

Wayne Dunkley #12 9
Bruce MacRae #35..13
Larry Smith #22 19
Denny Hrycaiko #25 25

Mel Smith #24...31
Jeannot Rodrigue #73..37
Brian Gervais #75..43
John Buda #66...49

Ole Hensrud #52..55
Cam Innes #40 61
Keith Johnston #55..67
Wayne Conrad #55 73

Dan Dulmage #63..91
Paul Kilger #74..97
John Danaher #64 101
Max Abraham #9 107

George Hill #26 113
Gill Bramwell #31 119
Bob Eccles #34 125
Glenn Ponomarenko #73 131

Bob Mincarelli #28 137
Rick Chevers #33 143
Chris Harber #8 145
Dave Kates #22 149

The End Zone 151

Introduction

The Search for the First CIS All-Canadian Football Team

An Unexpected Phone Call

On Saturday morning, November 20, 1971, I was just finishing my breakfast at my aunt's house in Dundas, Ontario when the phone rang. It was Doug Cihocki, a good friend who was studying at the University of Western Ontario and playing football for the UWO Mustangs. Doug had spent the night in Hamilton with his family and was preparing to leave for Toronto where the Western Mustangs were taking on the University of Alberta Golden Bears in the Vanier Cup, the national championship of college football in Canada.

Doug was calling to congratulate me on being selected to the All-Canadian football team.

I didn't understand what he was saying at first, and when it finally registered, I asked him how he knew, as I had heard nothing. He told me that it was in the morning paper. After thanking him for the call and wishing him luck in the Vanier Cup, I hung up and immediately called my dad in Dallas.

The Poster

The next week I received a call from McMaster's Football Coach, Ray Johnson, asking me to come to the gym to have my photo taken for a poster to commemorate the All Canada Football Team. Sometime in the next few weeks, a 16" by 20" poster arrived with a photo of each of the 24 members of the "1971 Intercollegiate – All Canada Football Team."

Several years passed, and the poster gathered dust in my closet. I finally had it framed and hung it on my wall, much to the chagrin of my wife. It has been hanging somewhere in my house ever since.

Over the past 45 years, I have looked at that poster hundreds of times and wondered what had happened to the other 23 members of that All-Star Team.

The First CIS All Canada Football Team

In the fall of 2006, I had an opportunity to attend a McMaster football game in Hamilton. The program had been going through a resurgence under the direction of Athletic Director Therese Quigley and Head Football Coach Greg Marshall. As I entered the game, I noticed that they were selling McMaster football media guides. I bought one and quickly found a page listing all of the McMaster football players who had ever been selected All-Canadian. I was shocked to see my name at the top of the list. I knew McMaster had been playing football for many years before I showed up in 1971, and I also knew that Russ Jackson had played for McMaster, so how was it that my name was the first on the list?

After doing a little research, I discovered that the CIS was formed in the late 1960s and had not selected an All Canada Football Team prior to 1971. I later discovered that Sports Canada magazine had selected an All Canada team in 1969, and Canadian Sports Digest had named a team in 1970. The next year, McMaster amended their media guide to include Joe Watt's name. Joe was selected first team All Canada in 1969 and 1970.

A Desire to Connect

In July 2016, I decided to satisfy my curiosity and see if I could at least find the other four offensive linemen from that team. I started my search for John Buda, Wayne Conrad, Cam Innes, and Ole Hensrud. I figured between Google, LinkedIn, and Facebook I should be able to track these guys down. After a few weeks of searching, I located John (an offensive tackle from the University of Waterloo) in Salmon Arm, BC, approximately 45 minutes from Vernon, BC, where I was living. Unfortunately, it took another two months before John and I would meet as he was in the process of moving from Salmon Arm to Calgary.

The First Meeting

In early October, John and I finally met for dinner in Calgary. We talked football for an hour and a half, conjuring up past memories of success and failure on the football field and reflecting on the impact playing football had had on our lives and our careers.

After a meal and a couple of beers, John suggested that we try to find the other 22 members of the 1971 All Canada Football Team. I told him, "Hell, John, it took me two months to find you," but he persisted, saying, "No, no. It'll be fun. We could all get together and meet at the Vanier Cup."

We agreed to give it a try and started looking for the other 22 guys the very next week.

My Old Friend Doug Cihocki

I thought the first place to start would be with Doug Cihocki. The University of Western had won the Vanier Cup in 1971, and as a result, the members of that team reunited at least every five years. I knew from my frequent conversations with Doug that he would know how to locate Dan Dulmage, George Hill, and Bruce MacRae, all of whom represented the UWO on the 1971 All Canada team.

Doug came through as expected with emails and phone numbers. Within a week, I had contacted the three Mustangs and became more optimistic about finding the rest of the players on that team.

Two Coaches—Frank Cosentino and Jim Donlevy

In my interview with George Hill, he mentioned Frank Cosentino, his coach at Western. By the time we finished the interview, George was encouraging me to talk to Frank and offered to connect us. He told me that Frank had written a number of books about sports in Canada and could probably provide another perspective on the 1971 season. Within a week, I was talking to Frank, and he graciously offered to write the foreword to this book.

In the process of uncovering some information on teammate Dave Kates, I was led to Bob Keating, who was a teammate of Gill Bramwell's at the University of Manitoba and played on both of the Bison's Vanier Cup teams in 1969 and 1970. Bob may be the only player in Canada with three Vanier Cup rings as he transferred to the University of Alberta and played on their Vanier Cup championship team in 1972. Bob played with Dave Kates and for Jim Donlevy. He shared his memories of Dave with me and then directed me to Jim Donlevy was selected as the coach of the year in 1971 as he coached the University of Alberta Golden Bears to their Vanier Cup encounter with Frank

Cosentino's University of Western Ontario Mustangs. Jim was able to fill in some of the gaps regarding Dave and added some of his own memories of the early 70s in Canadian university football.

With a Name Like Ponomarenko...

My next step was to look for Glenn Ponomarenko. I figured a name like that would be easy to find on Google or LinkedIn...and I was right. Within a few minutes of searching, I found Glenn in Winnipeg. He had recently retired from a very successful career in real estate. I made a few phone calls, and in time, I was talking to Glenn. He and I connected instantly. In fact, I call Glenn on a regular basis, particularly when I need a few laughs and to talk to someone who is extremely positive.

Glenn gave me some clues on how to find Max Abraham, one of his teammates from the University of Saskatchewan, and I was on to my next target.

Meeting for the First Time

I really didn't know how I would be received when I called these guys, whom I had never met, or at least never met formally. I'm pretty sure I bumped into Bob Eccles, Paul Kilger, George Hill, and John Buda once or twice during the 1971 season as I had played against all of them. I particularly remember Bob Eccles and John Buda, though. Bob because Ray Johnson had pointed out that Bob had been in the Ottawa Rough Riders camp in 1970. This shocked me as I could not understand how a university player could have been in a pro camp. I told John that I had a vivid memory of breaking the huddle in Waterloo and seeing him standing in the middle of the defensive line. Oh. My. God! I had never seen anybody that big across the line from me... it was a long night. Paul Kilger was another story, so keep reading.

Enthusiastic Response

Glenn Ponomarenko was not the only positive response I received to my phone calls; in fact, I was greeted warmly by everyone I spoke to. Several of these men wondered how I was able to find them, and almost all of them still had their posters. Those who didn't have it hanging on the wall dug it up and took another look at the 23 other players. No one realized that the 1971 team was the first CIS All Canada team.

The warm response was a little bit of a surprise to me as I had always worked myself up for games by demonizing my opponents. I guess 45 years have melted away any temporarily ill feelings we might've once had. I also discovered that several members of the '71 team had played for more than one university. This almost never happens in the U.S., which tends to prolong rivalries. And, of course, a bunch of men in their late sixties don't have the same testosterone levels as they did in their early twenties.

Help from the Universities

I thought I could get some help from the alma maters of some of the players, so I started calling the schools. In some cases, I received enthusiastic support and even a willingness to bypass some privacy rules to help me connect.

I spoke to someone in alumni relations at Carleton University and quickly received contact information for Bob Eccles and Chris Harber. I was equally successful with St. Francis Xavier as Bob Mincarelli had recently been inducted into their Sports Hall of Fame. They were able to furnish me with Bob's phone number and email address, which still reflects his association with StFX, including 'xmen' and his jersey number.

The Kinesiology Department at the University of Manitoba helped me find Gill Bramwell, Dennis Hrycaiko, and Ole Hensrud, although John Buda was able to make the first connection with Ole. I was able to get information on Mel Smith and Dave Kates from a combination of contacts at the University of Alberta and a friend of mine from Houston, Texas, who had played for the University of Alberta in the early 70s. Unfortunately, we discovered that Dave Kates had passed away in 2010.

Amazing Stories that Need to Be Remembered

I can't remember exactly when I got the idea to capture the lives of 24 football players in a book, but as the amazing stories began to unfold, I decided it would be a shame not to immortalize these stories. I called John Buda to discuss the idea, and he expressed his concern that we not commercialize this experience. I calmed his fears by telling him that it would not matter to me if I only distributed 24 copies. The book would be something for the players and their families to hold onto, and perhaps one or two of the universities might find a place for it in their archives. Along with the idea for a book, I also added a page to my website with photos and quotes from everyone I talked to:

www.truleadership.com/1971-cis-all-canada-football-team/

Canada 411

I wish I had a dime for each time I used 411 to try to find a member of the team. Fortunately, this approach produced results, most notably Paul Kilger. I was delighted to find Paul as I've been frustrated for 45 years by the fact that I never got a chance to face him one-on-one. When I told him this, he jokingly asked me if he was receiving a 'revenge call.'

Paul led me to Cam Innes because he and Cam had coached together at the University of Ottawa. I would never have found him without Paul's help as Cam had moved to Houston, Texas. Paul also let me know that Jeannot Rodrigue had passed away in 2014.

There must be something about defensive tackles because I also found John Danaher through 411. I believe John Buda found Wayne Dunkley through these listings as well. He and Wayne were in Stampeder camp together in 1973.

Relatives and Google

Using the information provided by Glenn Ponomarenko, I knew that Max Abraham was in the Saskatoon area and had taught school there as well. Since I had a cousin who spent the better part of her teaching career in Saskatoon, I took a chance and reached out to her. Sure enough, she pointed me directly to Max. I was getting closer to the end.

We reached out to the players we had already found to locate some of the remaining men. Unfortunately, with his first try, Glenn

Ponomarenko found an obituary for Rick Chevers. Given that result, Glenn said he didn't want to try to find anyone else.

I abandoned 411 in my search for Brian Gervais because there were simply too many of those in Canada. Brian had played for Dalhousie, so I was searching for him in the east. When I quit using 411, I turned to Google and found a story about him delivering a sermon in Lethbridge, Alberta. The article mentioned that he lived in Abbotsford, BC, which narrowed my search considerably. It only took a few phone calls to locate him after that.

Dealing with the Canadian Government

The hunt for Larry Smith turned out to be one of the more interesting searches. It wasn't difficult to find information on Larry as he had a long career with the Montreal Alouettes, had been their president and CEO, and also served as the CFL Commissioner for a number of years. It did take a little longer to realize that Larry was currently serving as a senator in the Canadian federal government. A few phone calls and emails sent to Ottawa produced results. I connected with Larry's assistant who provided me with his phone number. I had to work my way onto his schedule and was finally surprised to receive his "Larry Smith here" call while eating breakfast one Tuesday morning.

The Montreal Alouettes and Wayne Conrad

I had just about given up hope of finding Wayne when I read an article about how the Montreal Alouettes had a memorial for Tony Proudfoot and how Wayne had been a part of that memorial. I figured if the Alouettes had been able to find him in 2010, they might be able to find him now. I logged into the Alouette website and sent an email to their back office. I received an email from Wayne two days later.

The journey was over.

Wayne Dunkley #12

University of Toronto – Quarterback
First Team All-Canadian – 1971

Wayne was born and raised in Toronto and attended and played football for Monarch Park Collegiate. He didn't start playing football until he was in grade 11, so he only had a couple of years to play high school ball.

On Coaches and Coaching

Wayne holds his high school coaches in very high regard, saying:

> My high school coaches, who probably had the greatest impact on me, were outstanding. These guys taught the principles of playing and the ethics of the game. They were special people and had more influence on me than the game itself. I was a very fortunate athlete.

Later, he chose to play for the University of Toronto because some of his high school coaches were U of T PHE grads. When he went to U of T, he was fortunate again to play for another group of high quality coaches. He spoke specifically of Dave Copp, the team's offensive coordinator:

> Dave was a sensitive and understanding coach who was very protective of the position and image of the quarterback within the team. He was able to promote the position and the leadership aspect of it.

Good coaches appreciate and are prepared to protect the image of their quarterbacks. This includes not criticizing them in public and taking them aside to discuss their mistakes. Wayne laughed as he indicated that this happened to him frequently:

In front of the team, you were given every opportunity to develop leadership in whatever capacity you could: the way you played, the way you spoke to the team, etc. It's an invaluable aspect of coaching as far as all athletes are concerned. This approach is something that I took with me when I coached high school sports and into my job as an athletic coordinator. These are things I learned not necessarily from football itself, but from the coaching of the game, and would apply to any other sport. Coaches need to be able to develop the self-confidence of their athletes if they are going to be truly successful. Coaches need to make this a priority, especially in practices where the whole team is there and observing what is going on.

Wayne's primary memories of the 1971 season were of his coaches and teammates. He remembers the camaraderie and the fun but not many details from the games themselves. He did remember beating Western in 1971 and then seeing them go on to win the College Bowl. He also remembers that the coaches at U of T put in the shotgun offense in 1971 because Wayne had lost some mobility due to injury, which he said was "innovative at the time and made games and practices very exciting."

Thoughts about Being Selected for an All-Star Team

For Wayne, being selected to the All-Canadian football team was an honor, but he made it clear that he puts very little stock in individual awards and recognition in football, "Especially for the position of quarterback, whose success is almost totally dependent on the skills of the offensive line. Football is a team sport."

He went on to elaborate about the quarterback's dependency on the offensive line. When I asked if he would do anything differently if he had the chance, Wayne said, "Yes! I would have begged the offensive line much harder for more time, just one more second on each pass play, and perhaps now I wouldn't be agreeing that 'the older we get, the better we were.'" Wayne believes that what makes quarterbacks perform differently comes down to how much time they have to find their receivers.

> "That one extra second in the pocket can make the difference between completing one pass and competing a lot of passes."

What Wayne had to say about the quarterback position could be said about almost any position. Great linebackers will make a lot of tackles if the defensive linemen in front of them are able to keep the offensive linemen from reaching them. Receivers make a lot more catches when the ball is thrown on time and where they can get to it. Running backs need holes to run through, and offensive linemen are only as good as the men beside them. If one lineman gets his block but the guy beside him misses his, the quarterback is sacked, or the running back is thrown for a loss, and it really doesn't matter if he got his block or not. Football truly is the ultimate team sport.

The Quarterback's Perspective

Wayne expressed delight at the interaction between the various members of the 1971 All Canada team, particularly that between opposing positions:

> "Quarterbacks aren't going head-to-head with someone on every play like linemen are. They're dealing with concepts half the time."

I shared some of my other interviews with Wayne, and he found it interesting to read the feedback going back and forth among us. He said, "It's a different perspective entirely. It's kind of neat that after 45 years, and after banging heads on the football field, you guys can get together to work on a project."

Career

No one can encapsulate another athlete's career and experience directly. When I asked Wayne to tell me his story, he shared the following with me:

> I was drafted by Calgary, attended camp, and met John Buda and the others. It was an interesting, but short experience, lasting only four days. Several of the Canadian kids walked out and went to Banff Springs. For me, I felt that I could throw the ball and understood the game as well as the American quarterbacks but realistically lacked many of the finer skills necessary to play at that level. Like most Canadian quarterbacks, I would have been a project for the coaching staff. When I was asked to step in as a defensive back, I knew it was time to step away. A beer with the boys in Banff was a good alternative.

I returned to U of T for my final year and prepared myself for a career in Education. The school where I began my teaching career was only blocks from U of T, and I was able to act as an assistant coach for the next eight years. It was a great experience and allowed me to give back to the program.

Wayne also recalled a time when he was coaching at the University of Toronto in 1974:

We were getting ready to play the Ottawa Gee-Gees. We had our entire offensive strategy for the game built around neutralizing Paul Kilger, an outstanding defensive tackle who was selected to the 1971 All-Canadian Football Team and the 1975 All-Canadian team. Wayne said they tried double-teaming Paul, trapping him and doing whatever they could to keep him off guard. They wanted to see to it that Paul didn't know whether he was coming or going. He added that Paul still had a hell of a game.

Wayne enjoyed a 35-year career as a Physical Education teacher and athletic director and "continued [his] involvement in sports as the Athletic Coordinator for the Conference Independent Schools of Ontario for seven years."

Would You Do It Again?

It sounds like a simple question, but after all my searching to find these gentlemen, it was one that I felt compelled to ask. I was anxious to learn if everyone else loved the game like I did...and missed it as much as I do. I also felt like the question would reveal some insights about each member of the team. Wayne's response:

"You're darn right, I would. I can say this even after major surgeries on both ankles."

Where Is He Now?

Wayne is retired now and living in Whitby, Ontario. He still sees his former coaches from U of T on a regular basis. Ron Murphy, Dave Copp, and the others join Wayne each year for a golf outing and a weekend away at the family cottage or a resort.

Bruce MacRae #35

University of Western Ontario – Running Back
First Team All-Canadian – 1971

Bruce was born in Toronto and moved to Port Credit (now Mississauga) when he was five-years-old. He started playing football while attending Port Credit High School.

Loving the Game Despite Heart Breaking Losses

I loved the game. We lost three consecutive Toronto Township championships during the three years I played senior ball in high school. My last year, 1968, I also played in the first Toronto East/West Football High School All-Star Contest. I don't remember much about the game other than it was a really tough battle.

Coaches and the Road to University of Western Ontario

Bruce describes his high school football coach, Murray Hadlow, as a great coach and teacher.

I will always remember his tryout with the Toronto Rifles in the new Continental League at age 30. He was married and had a couple of kids. He hadn't played in 10 years but wanted to give it one last shot. Pretty impressive.

Bruce also benefited from an opportunity to work out with a number of Argos who had chosen his high school for their spring workouts. His success as a high school football player resulted in a scholarship to play for Simon Fraser University in British Columbia, but after attending training camp, he realized that the school wasn't for him.

An assistant coach at Port Credit, Peter Martin, a Western alumni and linebacker for the Toronto Argonauts, introduced Bruce and some of his teammates to John Metras, the head coach from the University of Western Ontario. Coach Metras visited with Bruce and his mother at their Port Credit residence while he was mulling over a few scholarship offers. As a result of his contact with Coach Metras, Bruce applied and was accepted to the University of Western Ontario. When he made the decision to leave Simon Fraser, he reached out to see if he could still play for Western. Coach Metras responded quickly and set him up to room with a former high school teammate, Steve Derbyshire, who had also declined a scholarship offer from Simon Fraser and opted for Western.

Playing for the Mustangs – Off to a Rocky Start

Bruce had a successful first year with the Mustangs in 1968, becoming a starting running back out of the blocks, but an industrial accident during a summer job resulted in a crushed hand, loss of his middle finger on his right hand, and a missed football season in 1969. He was nevertheless quite fortunate as the surgeon on duty at the hospital had recommended that his arm be amputated just below the elbow. Fortunately, Bruce's stepmom had family connections, and an alternative surgeon was able to save his arm.

In the fall of 1970, Bruce was back in uniform but was injured in an exhibition game against Queens and missed the entire season.

> I was on the punting team and was first downfield to meet the punt returner. I foolishly lowered my head and met the runner as his knee was coming up. We were both badly hurt; I couldn't move and was paralyzed for a few hours having compressed a disk in my neck. I could subsequently walk but not much else for several months. But I count myself lucky as the end result could have been much worse.

1971 – A National Championship – A Tale of Two Seasons

When Bruce returned in 1971 he felt he was "good to go, but it took a few games to get re-acclimated after missing a couple of years." The Mustangs seemed to reflect Bruce's condition as the team got off to a slow start that season.

> I spent a couple of games on the bench, a first for me and a humbling experience at the time, but in hindsight [it was] appropriate. Sitting on the bench propelled me to work harder.

John Metras, who had been like a stern father figure to Bruce, retired after the 1969 season. Frank Cosentino, the new head coach, after a distinguished 10-year CFL career as a quarterback, brought a different perspective to the game with new ideas and philosophies.

> Frank brought us all into the new age of football.

The Mustangs were a mediocre team for the first half of the season, but their turning point came when they lost to McMaster on a last second field goal. It was an extremely humid day in early October with the temperature reaching 85 degrees. Both teams were listless for most of the second half, but the Mustangs took a 16–14 lead at the 11:15 mark in the fourth quarter. McMaster mounted a sustained drive in the closing minutes and kicked the winning field goal as time ran out. McMaster had missed the field goal the play before, but Western was offside on the play giving McMaster a second chance five yards closer.

After the following Monday's practice, the players decided to have a private meeting. All the tensions between the team and the coaching staff and among the players themselves were brought out in the open. Later that night, team captain George Hill approached Cosentino to say that the team members were unhappy with the fact that the starting defensive and offensive units scrimmaged only against utility players in practices and that it kept the units apart and destroyed any feeling of cohesiveness. Cosentino adjusted the practice routine in line with their wishes.

The players responded. In Cosentino's words, "Whether that change had any bearing on the final outcome of our season, I guess

I'll never really know. But one thing is for certain—from that point on we never looked back."

The Mustangs went on to clinch their division after that loss and stormed into the playoffs after a meaningless loss to the University of Windsor. According to teammate and fellow All-Canadian George Hill, Bruce was 'a beast' during the playoffs. He carried the ball 95 times in four games for 445 yards, just short of five yards per carry. The Mustangs won the College Bowl on a last second field goal by Paul Knill against the University of Alberta.

Football After University – A Path to a Career

Bruce was drafted by the Calgary Stampeders and attended their training camp in the summer of 1972.

> I had a reasonable camp but was not included in their final plans to start the season, so I decided to leave, come back to London, Ontario, and play for the Senior ORFU London Lords. The Lords had assembled a terrific team in anticipation of acquiring a CFL franchise that never materialized. Halfway through the season, I severely injured my left knee in a game against Buffalo...that was the end of football for me.

On the bright side, though, Bruce benefited from the Lords' job referral placement program. He ended up working for the Bank of Montreal, and he is still with one of their group companies, BMO Nesbitt Burns.

Taking the Good with the Bad

Bruce's worst personal memory from that season was pining for another opportunity to get back into the game after cooling his heels on the bench for a couple of games. When that final moment arrived, it became a wonderfully positive experience. Today, his worst memories "pertain to the nine comrades who have passed on, most recently Quarterback Joe Fabiani in the spring of 2016."

Would You Do It Again?

> Absolutely! The skills learned in a very competitive, team oriented environment help transition us to our daily life experiences and successes. Other than a couple of knee operations, I wouldn't/couldn't replace the positive memories.

Bruce contends that his life experiences were highly impacted by his football experience.

> Certainly, there is a strong correlation between hard work and success, overcoming adversity, the need for collaboration, understanding your role and those of your teammates, mutual respect, etc. It all ties together.

When asked if he would do anything differently Bruce's first reaction was to say that he thought he would have spent more time on his studies and cut back on the partying…"But then again, probably not."

A Great Group of Guys

Because they won the College Bowl, the 1971 Mustang Football Team has stayed in touch throughout all these years.

> We have a great group of guys and have grown closer over the years, recognizing that time is indeed limited. We keep in touch through our leader George Hill, play golf with several teammates a couple of times a year, and recently attended Homecoming and celebrated our 45th College Bowl anniversary.

Where Is He Now?

Bruce married his college sweetheart, Barbara and has lived in Oakville since 1983. They have two children and have been blessed with one granddaughter. He's in good health and is still working as an Investment Advisor with BMO Nesbitt Burns in downtown Toronto.

THE END COMES QUICK

Larry Smith #22

Bishop's University – Running Back
First Team All-Canadian 1969 and 1971

From a very early age, anyone who knew **Larry** could see that he was destined to play football for the Montreal Alouettes. Little did they realize that he would not only play for them, but he would also go on to be their president and ultimately become the Commissioner of the Canadian Football League.

Growing Up as an Alouettes Fan

Larry says that he grew up in Montreal following the Alouettes, and, in particular, their two running backs, Don Clark and George Dixon, from the early 1960s.

> My dad bought me an Alouettes football helmet when I started playing sandlot football at the age of seven. I had a brother who was three and half years older than me, and I used to tag along with him to play football with him and his friends. Given that they were a lot older and a lot bigger, I got the crap beaten out of me on a regular basis.

Larry was not the only Alouettes fan in the family. His parents had season tickets to games from 1950 until his mother gave them up in 2007.

Small but Mighty

Larry attended Hudson High School, which was a small school with only 300 students. Despite the school's size, they had a competitive football program and won the city championship in Montreal during Larry's senior year. They played Westhill High School, which was several times Hudson's size. Since the Hudson bench was pretty thin, 12 of the 19 players on the team were two-way starters.

> The Westhill fans arrived at the championship game in 20 school buses, and the Hudson fans arrived in three. We won the game by a score of 18–13. I had a good game, rushing for more than 100 yards and scoring three touchdowns.

Moving on to Bishop's

Larry had opportunities to play football for several universities, but since his grandfather, his uncle, and his brother all went to Bishop's University, you might have said it was easy to follow in their footsteps.

Bruce Coulter was the coach at Bishop's and had played 10 seasons for the Montreal Alouettes, including the Grey Cup championship season in 1949. He then went on to coach 29 seasons for the Bishop's Gaiters. Larry had a great deal of respect for Bruce and described him as a "great coach." Bruce was able to help Larry become one of the premier running backs in Canadian college football.

Larry recalls the 1969 season at Bishop's as his best year rushing as a Gaiter. He rushed for 1050 yards that year, and Bishop's made it into the playoffs, losing to Windsor in the early rounds. *Sports Canada Magazine* selected him to the All-Canadian team that year as well.

The 1971 season saw the Gaiters complete a perfect 6–0 conference schedule that earned them the conference championship, but they lost to the University of Alberta Golden Bears in the Western Bowl, which ended their season and Larry's last year as a Gaiter. He finished the season as one of the top running backs in Canada, was selected to the first CIS All Canada Football Team, and was projected to be selected in the first round of the CFL draft.

The Fumble and Destiny

The Toronto Argonauts played the Calgary Stampeders in the 1971 Grey Cup at Empire Stadium in Vancouver, and the outcome would affect the Canadian college draft the next season. In the last few minutes of the game, Toronto defender, Dick Thornton, a great two-way player who had already made a fantastic reception, intercepted a Calgary pass and returned it to the Stampeder 11-yard line. With Theismann back in the game, he handed the ball off to Leon McQuay, the Argonauts' star running back. As McQuay cut left across the field, he promptly slipped on the soggy turf and fumbled the ball, which was recovered by Stampeder Reggie Holmes. This sealed the victory for Calgary and at the same time gave the fortuitous first draft pick to the Montreal Alouettes...and they chose Larry.

A Lengthy Career with the Alouettes

Larry not only made the Alouettes roster in 1972, he became the first Canadian to become a starting running back in the Canadian Football League since Ronnie Stewart, the Hall of Fame Ottawa Rough Rider. In his early years with Montreal, he was primarily a running back, but in later years he showed his versatility and was used primarily as a receiver coming out of the backfield.

In total, Larry played nine seasons for the Alouettes and has great stats:

- 140 consecutive regular season games
- 13 playoff games
- 5 Grey Cup games

He helped the Als win the Grey Cup in 1974 and 1977 and racked up 1,696 rushing yards on 397 carries for an average of 4.3 yards per carry as well as eight touchdowns. He also caught 238 passes for 2,772 yards and 18 touchdowns.

A Successful and Varied Business Career

Larry earned his Bachelor of Arts degree in Economics from Bishop's in 1972 and then continued his studies at McGill University while playing for the Als. He earned his Bachelors of Civil Law degree in 1976.

He began his business career during his playing days, working in sales, marketing, and human resources. In 1983, Larry joined Industrial Life Technical Services as general manager of the Montreal branch. He took over the multi-products division in 1984 and became senior vice president of the Central Region just a year later. From 1985 to 1992, Larry held several executive positions within John Labatt Ltd, and he was president of the frozen bakery division of Ogilvie Mills Ltd. before he became CFL Commissioner in 1992. Stepping into this position enabled Larry to do something many former athletes only dream of—combining their love of the game of football with their career.

Larry was the CFL Commissioner from 1992 to 1997, during which time he oversaw the expansion of the CFL into the U.S. In 1997 he became the President and CEO of the Montreal Alouettes after the team was re-established in Montreal, having been absent for nine years. Larry was the man behind moving the Baltimore Stallions, one of the U.S. expansion teams, to Montreal in 1996 and took over as president at the urging of the club's new owner. He served as president and CEO from 1997 until 2001, and then again from 2004 to 2010. During the years in between he was president and publisher of the Montreal Gazette newspaper.

Reflecting on His Career, Young Players, and Today's Fans and Critics

When asked if he would do it all again, Larry paused and then said he would be a lot more careful the next time around.

> Playing in the CFL takes quite a toll on your body. It can be very intimidating in the pros.

Larry recalled a time early in his career with the Als when they ran a "sucker trap," which was supposed to pull the linebacker and leave a hole for the running back to get through. On this particular play, the linebacker was not fooled and met Larry in the hole. It was quite an introduction to the pros.

He says that he advises parents to not let their sons start playing football until they are 14 or 15 years old, adding, "They should play a sport like soccer, not football, until their bodies mature."

Larry also feels that fans and sports writers should not compare today's players to those from the past. He says, "The game is different now; the players are different."

Retiring from the CFL

When Larry finally stepped down from his job with the Alouettes and began another chapter in his life, he was asked why he had chosen that particular moment to walk away from the team and the CFL:

> Every good thing comes to an end. We accomplished a lot in Montreal. I think we helped the CFL put itself in a better position, and sometimes you make decisions to go on with your life. I'd like to do some different things. [It's] been a great ride, but [it was] time to move on.

Larry was also asked about the best way for people to describe him, as a former football player or a former executive. He responded by saying:

> I never felt that football as a sport defined who I was. I have a great family. I'm blessed that I've had the support from my wife to do pretty well what I wanted to do. But I think my strength, if I have one, is what they call in French being a rassembleur—someone who can get people to follow a vision, get people involved to try and work and build things. That's been my life.

Life in Politics

On December 18, 2010, Larry was summoned to the Canadian Senate on the advice of Prime Minister Stephen Harper and sat as a conservative. Following an unsuccessful run for parliament, Larry was reappointed to the Senate in May 2011 and is currently serving as a senator, where his duties include overseeing budget adherence by different factions of the government.

Where Is He Now?

Larry and his wife Leesa reside in Hudson, Quebec. They have three children, two sons and a daughter, and two grandchildren.

Larry's son Brad was an All-Canadian at Queens University, which means that Larry and Brad are one of only two father-son combinations to earn recognition as All-Canadian football players. The other combination being Neil Lumsden and his son Jesse.

Larry had the pleasure of coaching Brad and his team to a city championship when Brad was in high school. Brad played in the CFL for five years as a receiver with the Toronto Argonauts and Edmonton Eskimos.

Denny Hrycaiko #25

University of Manitoba – Halfback
First Team All-Canadian – 1971

"I am a Winnipeg Guy"

Denny was born in St. Boniface Hospital, now a part of Winnipeg, and other than three years at the University of Alberta and three years at the University of Windsor he has spent his whole life in Winnipeg.

He played football in his neighborhood growing up and started playing six-man football for the Broadway Optimist Community Club at 13.

> We had a strong team and were always competitive. In my third and final year, we won the City of Winnipeg Six-Man Football Championship for the 15-year-old category.

Denny played high school football for Grant Park High School. His first year at Grant Park he was still playing for Broadway Optimist, so he only played two years for the Grant Park Pirates.

In all his years playing six-man football, and for Grant Park, Denny played both ways. He was a defensive back and a halfback on offense. In his final year at Grant Park, he was selected to the Winnipeg High School All-Star Team as an offensive back. In 1992, Denny was selected to the Grant Park Hall of Fame, to the Winnipeg High School Football Hall of Fame (player category) in 2008, and the Grant Park Football Hall of Fame in 2014.

Junior Football and University of Manitoba

Denny started playing for the Weston Wildcats of the Manitoba/Saskatchewan Junior Football League in 1965. He played for three years and was selected to the conference all-star team as an offensive back in both 1966 and 1967. While still playing for the Wildcats, Denny enrolled at the University of Winnipeg. After completing his eligibility in junior football, he moved on to the University of Manitoba after being accepted into the physical education degree program in 1968 and started playing football for coach and athletic director Henry Janzen. He completed his degree in three years and then enrolled in the Faculty of Education program to get his teacher's certificate and played a fourth year for the Bisons.

Henry Janzen and Denny's Coaching Career

Denny played his entire four years at the University of Manitoba for Coach Henry Janzen. He speaks fondly of Janzen and credits him with having an enormous impact on his life.

> The four years I played for him were great years. We had four really good football teams, winning two Vanier Cups and appearing in the Western Canadian Intercollegiate Athletic Association (W.C.I.A.A.) final on two other occasions (1968 and 1971). Henry was such a nice person, and, of course, he was an outstanding football player himself, having played six years with the Winnipeg Blue Bombers.

Henry was not just Denny's football coach: "As a professor, he took me under his wing, guided me along, and gave me lots of encouragement. He was the one who convinced me to go to graduate school."

In 1972, Denny started his teaching and coaching career at Westdale School in Winnipeg. During that year, he accepted an offer from Head Coach George Motoch of the Winnipeg Hawkeyes Juvenile Football Club to join his team as offensive coordinator and to install the Bison offense. The Hawkeyes had a solid team, an explosive offense, and a tough defense. They won the Canadian Juvenile Football Championship in 1972. For the next nine years, Denny's career path took him away from Winnipeg and the borders of Manitoba (1973-1979).

But in 1979, Henry Janzen convinced him to come back to the University of Manitoba as the head football coach. Following the 1971 season, Henry had stepped down from his coaching/athletic director position and became the dean of the faculty. Denny proudly recalls, "He was so happy to have me take over as the head football coach."

Denny was the Bison's head football coach for 11 seasons. During those years, they had two very strong teams. The 1979 and 1985 teams both made it to the Western Intercollegiate Football League (WIFL) final, losing to Alberta in 1979 and Calgary in 1985. (Note: WIFL replaced WCIAA and is now called Canada West). Denny was among the first inductees to the Football Manitoba Hall of Fame in the coach category in 2010.

After stepping down from his head coaching responsibilities, Denny focused his time on his role as Associate Dean (Academic), but also devoted two seasons to helping his former teammate, Gill Bramwell (a fellow 1971 All-Canadian), get the football program at Oak Park High School off the ground. By the way, Oak Park won the Winnipeg high school championship in their third season.

Denny still meets with Henry Janzen every couple of weeks. "We get together with our wives to have coffee."

Football Memories

During his four years with the Bisons, Denny played in three Western Bowl finals and two Vanier Cups. The Bisons were the first team to win back-to-back championships, and the two Vanier Cup teams were inducted into the Football Manitoba Hall of Fame in 2012. Denny recalls the pain of losing to Queens in the Western Bowl final in 1968 but praised the quality of the Queens team. He also regrets losing to Alberta in 1971 and missing an opportunity to play in three consecutive Vanier Cups:

> I was the W.C.I.A.A. nominee for the Hec Crighton Award in 1968, and I represented my team (U of M) for the award again in 1971. I was a late round draft choice of the Blue Bombers after the 1970 season. Winnipeg offered me $3,500, so I decided to go back to school to get my teaching certificate and play another year of football for the Bisons.

Graduate Programs

After obtaining his teaching certificate in Education while teaching at Westdale School, Denny applied for graduate school at the University of Alberta and was accepted. He started his master's degree program in July 1973.

> I completed the Master of Arts and Physical Education degree program in one calendar year, and my advisor invited me to continue on in my doctoral studies. I started my doctorate in the fall of 1974 and completed it in 1976. Basically, I was a full-time student. I wanted to get in and out of there quickly.

Upon completion of his doctoral degree, Denny was offered a job as an assistant professor and head wrestling coach at the University of Windsor. He stayed there for three years and then returned to the University of Manitoba in 1979 to become assistant professor and head football coach.

Wrestling – Competing Against a World Champion

During his final year in the Physical Education degree program at the U of M, Denny entered an intramural wrestling tournament and won his weight class. "So, the last year at Manitoba, while I was working on my teaching certificate, I had quite a bit of time after football season, so I went out for the wrestling team."

While competing for the University of Manitoba, Denny had an opportunity to wrestle Michi Tanaka, a former world champion wrestler from Japan (1969) who was attending the University of Alberta:

> It was a great opportunity, but, of course, I got the worst of that one. I spent most of the first period bridging on the side of my face. I had no skin on my face by the time the period was over. He actually let me up at one point. I had been down for about a minute, and he couldn't pin me in the position he had me in. I wasn't up very long, and he had me down again, and this time he had me in a position where he could pin me. I did last longer against him than anyone in the tournament, though. It was a great wrestling experience.

Tanaka was the CIAU and Canadian Open Champion in his weight class in 1971.

When Denny applied for the graduate program at the University of Alberta he planned to play football. Unfortunately, the rules had changed, and he was not allowed to play a fifth year for a team other than the University of Manitoba. Denny's understanding was that the same rules did not apply to wrestling, so he went out for the U of A wrestling team. Tanaka was still there, so he got to know him quite well. The U of A team also had five Canadian national champions—which made for a great learning environment! After making the wrestling team, Denny was informed that the eligibility rules applied to all sports, including wrestling. Fortunately, the head wrestling coach allowed Denny to continue working out with his new teammates for the remainder of the season.

Long-Term Goals of Coaching

The next year they changed the head wrestling coach. John Barry, a teammate and national champion at the U of A, became the head coach and asked Denny to be his assistant. Being John's assistant (for two years) led to Denny's appointment as the head wrestling coach at the University of Windsor.

Denny had always wanted to coach. When the opportunity at the U of A developed, tied to a paid teaching assistantship within the doctoral program, it was too good to refuse. Within the assistantship, Denny would be the assistant wrestling coach and a guest coach in the football (fall and Spring) camps for football head coach Jim Donlevy. The football and wrestling coach positions fulfilled a goal and paved the way for a career in coaching.

Crossing Paths

Denny reflected on how he was able to cross paths with so many coaches and former football players throughout his career. While on staff at the University of Windsor, he helped legendary coach Gino Fracas with coaching and scouting. He got to know Gino well as a fellow staff member, and they became good friends. Gino would remark about how Denny had "put the dagger in us" with a long touchdown run in the 1969 Western Bowl when the Bisons defeated the University of Windsor on their way to their first Vanier Cup. "But, he then always laughed, because he saw us as good friends."

Denny worked with Cam Innes on the coaching steering committee while he was the head coach at Manitoba and Cam was the head coach for the University of Ottawa. Gino Fracas and Jim Donlevy were also in this group as well as other notable coaches across the country. Therein, lies the foundation of the football coaches' certification program of Canada.

While in school at the University of Alberta, Denny mingled with players who were his opponents a few years earlier and got to know Dan Syrotuik who had played for McMaster in 1971. Like Denny, Dan coached with the Bears and did his graduate study work with the Golden Bears of Alberta.

Would You Do It Again?

Although Denny lists his worst days as those when the Bisons lost to Queens in 1968 and the University of Alberta in 1971, he sums up his football career by saying, "I don't have any bad memories."

Where Is He Now?

Denny recently retired from the University of Manitoba, and is enjoying his retirement in the Winnipeg area.

Mel Smith #24

University of Alberta – Flanker
First Team All-Canadian 1970 and 1971

Mel was born and raised in Edmonton, and his entire football career took place in this city. He remembers playing bantam football when he was 13 or 14 years old. He moved on from bantam into high school and played all but one year. He sat out grade 11 due to injury.

The Impact of a High School Coach

I had a really great high school coach, Bob Dean, an old Eskimo. He took a bunch of us that could have gone either way, and he straightened a few of us out and got us going to school and working on something meaningful. He was a great coach and motivator. He recruited a bunch of guys from different parts of the city, and I think he won three championships in a row. I only played on one of those championship teams. He had quite an influence because he spent extra time with all of us and made sure we were doing the right things. He was a character but also a no-nonsense guy. He intimidated the shit out of all of us and was tougher than nails. I believe he played guard and linebacker for Edmonton. He had been an All-American volleyball player and football player in Maryland and came to Canada to play for the Eskimos and never went back."

Deciding on the Golden Bears

Coming out of high school, Mel was offered a scholarship to play for Simon Fraser University, but what they offered was not enough to offset the costs of moving to BC and living on campus. Mel's sister had attended the University of Alberta, and he knew some of the players in addition to being familiar with the Golden Bears football program, having grown up in Edmonton. The decision to stay home and play football for the Golden Bears was an easy one.

Playing for the Golden Bears

Mel's years with the Golden Bears were highlighted by two visits to the Vanier Cup, being named to two All Canada teams, and being awarded the Hec Crighton trophy in 1971 as Canada's most outstanding player in Canadian university football.

During his first year at the University of Alberta, he was one of four high school kids, all age 18 or 19, to make the team. He found it hard to adjust to playing with men who were 25 or 26 years old. In those days, athletes could play a sport for five years, and it did not matter when those five years took place.

In 1967, the University of Alberta played McMaster in the Vanier Cup. They won that game by a score of 10–9, stopping McMaster short of the goal line in the closing moments to clinch the victory.

Mel dropped out of school for a year in 1968 and played football for the Wildcats junior team in Edmonton.

> I had started in the engineering programme but was not focused, and my grades suffered. The coaches tried to talk me into switching into the Physical Education programme in 1968, but I wasn't doing that, so I took a year off. The next year I came back and enrolled in the science programme."

He recalls what it was like to play without any financial aid:

> One year the coaches let us eat dinner at one of the dorms a couple of nights a week. That was a big deal; I guess it was worth something. We ate them out of ice cream and cake and all the sweet stuff, but the rest of the food was awful. I'd rather have gone home. That was our scholarship. I used to tell the coach, 'This is punishment. You guys are only doing this so you can see who goes where.'"

The Golden Bears big rival was Calgary. Mel says, "We had to beat them. Manitoba had great teams in the 60s, so those games were always battles. In our conference, we usually played each team twice at home and away."

Mel believes his fourth year, 1970, was his best. He was selected to the All-Canadian team that year, and the selections were made by *Canadian Sports Digest*. Following the 1970 season, he was drafted by the Edmonton Eskimos.

Short Stint with the Eskimos

> I was the second-string receiver in the preseason and was also running back kicks. The coach asked me to drop a few pounds and move to wide receiver. I dropped from 208 to about 195, but I could see what was happening. I approached the coach who had recruited me and told him that I did not want to be on the roster for two games into the regular season and get cut. I still had one more year of college eligibility, and I would prefer to return to college for my final year rather than lose the season and not even play in the CFL.

The coach cut Mel, and he returned to the University of Alberta for his fifth year. He said that the player from Saskatchewan who took his place with the Eskimos was cut two games into the regular season. Coincidence?

The 1971 Vanier Cup

The Golden Bears only lost one game during the 1971 season and ultimately advanced to the Vanier Cup against the University of Western Ontario Mustangs. Memories of the '71 Vanier Cup are very painful for Mel. They lost that game 15–14 on a field goal in the closing seconds:

> I was upset about that game, and I still get mad when I think about it. We played on a muddy field, which neutralized all our outside speed. Our coach also changed up our offense for that game. He took out a bunch of stuff that we had been running all year and put in some new plays that really didn't work. We played a very conservative game. All year long we had spread people out across the field. The field conditions for that final game dictated our play, but I felt we could have done a lot more. A couple of our players were also hurt. It was a hard loss. For a lot of us, it was our last college game. That was a tough one.

The bright side: as many as eight players from that team went on to CFL camps the next fall.

Another Crack at the CFL

The good thing about being cut from the Eskimos in '71 was that I was a free agent in '72.

Jackie Parker had been one of Mel's idols when he was growing up. He had moved up to become the GM for the BC Lions, so when he called Mel about coming to BC for a tryout, Mel was quick to respond. He had been offered a contract by Edmonton, but BC offered more money, and when they threw in a $500 signing bonus he agreed to play for them.

> I went to their training camp and had a great camp. In fact, I don't think I dropped a single pass in two or three weeks. I never got to play for them, though, because they cut me right at the end of camp. I had nowhere to go, and I could not negotiate with anyone because they were all making their final cuts before the season started. A week or two later, Calgary phoned me.

Calgary was interested in taking a look at Mel. He returned to Alberta and spent two weeks on their taxi squad. Seeing that he was not going to make the team, he returned to Edmonton to look for a real job. It wasn't long after that when he received a call from Winnipeg. They had lost a player to injury and needed someone to fill his roster spot. They promised that if he came out to sign a contract they would keep him on the team for the rest of the season. Within a couple of weeks after joining the Bombers, the team experienced several more injuries, and as a result had to make some major roster changes. Mel was let go, thus ending his football career. He returned to Edmonton and looked for a career.

It was a bittersweet departure. Mel recalled seeing one of his teammates in Winnipeg suffer a career-ending knee injury right beside him on the field.

> I was running off the field after the play thinking to myself, 'This isn't that neat.' That guy was going to be crippled for a year or two and would never play the game again."

Career and Life Lessons from Football

Mel found a job working for one of the large financial institutions in Canada. He worked there for a couple years then spent 15 years in banking. He started with what was then the Bank of British Columbia and moved on to the Bank of Alberta. After that, he spent a couple years in his own business before moving into the automobile industry as a leasing specialist. He finished a 20-year career in leasing and retired at age 62. For the first five years of his retirement, he and his wife travelled to Palm Springs each winter for a few months, and Mel played a lot of golf.

When asked about what he took with him into the business world from football, Mel responded:

> You know, what you learn as an athlete is that you are going to lose. You learn that you have to get up and that there is always another play. In sales, we used to always laugh about how many times we were told 'No.' As a salesman, as in football, you have to keep going back and trying something different until you succeed. You make another offer or renegotiate the deal. You also learn from football not to be intimidated.

Jeannot Rodrigue #73

University of Ottawa – Receiver
First Team All-Canadian – 1971, 1972, and 1973

Sadness Along the Way

As I mentioned in the introduction, I wasn't able to speak with all the amazing men from the 1971 All-Canadian Team; some, sadly, had passed on. **Jeannot** was among those whose history I gratefully learned thanks to his family.

Among the Best Players of the Program's History

Jeannot Rodrigue was inducted into the University of Ottawa Gee-Gees Sports Hall of Fame in 2006. If you look him up on their website, this is what you'll find:

> Rodrigue had a successful football career with the University of Ottawa in the early 70s and is among the best players of the program's history. Rodrigue, who led his team as a captain from 1971 to 1973, was a 3-time OUAA All-Star and CIS All-Canadian, and one of the very rare players to be awarded each and every season of his career. Despite his undeniable talent and success, Jeannot's selfless and humble attitude has made him a true role model for his peers. He is one of the pillars of the University of Ottawa Gee-Gees football program and was inducted into the GGs Hall of Fame in 2006. Mr. Rodrigue has also been a highly-respected teacher and coach at Colonel By High School, where he spent most of his career before retiring in 2003.

Those who had the privilege of playing with Jeannot speak of him in glowing terms. From his accomplishments on the football field to what a pleasure he was to be around in the locker room; he was clearly one of the most revered players to ever put on a Gee-Gees uniform.

An Exceptional Athlete from an Early Age

Jeannot's father was in the Air Force, so they moved a lot when he was growing up. His brother, Moe, recalls the many moves they made in the early years:

> We started in Moncton, New Brunswick, and then we moved to Trenton, Ontario. From there we moved to Saskatoon, and finally back to Ottawa, where Mom and Dad were from. Dad retired from the Air Force and worked in government in Ottawa for about 10 years.

Jeannot's athleticism was evident at an early age. He started playing baseball when he was nine or ten years old. He was his team's starting pitcher, but he was also the team's leading hitter, well known for his ability to hit home runs. He was a baseball all-star, and he also played hockey for a couple of years and excelled in that sport as well.

Jeannot played basketball in high school in addition to football. He became an avid cyclist, touring Europe and even climbing Mount Ventoux, which is the most difficult hill to climb on the Tour de France. He even enjoyed cross country skiing. Willing to take on any challenge, and loving competition, Jeannot started playing tennis, and he and a friend won the doubles championship in Ottawa. He was an all-around athlete.

Football in High School and College

Jeannot played football for Rideau High School in Ottawa where his junior team won the city championship. According to his teammate, Bruce MacGregor, he was part of the key play in the championship game against Hillcrest:

> In the fourth quarter, the snap on a third down sailed over the head of kicker Tom Deacon. Deacon ran back and picked up the ball, then ran to his right, looked downfield, and heaved a desperation pass to Jeannot. This play set up what proved to be the winning touchdown in a one point victory."

At the end of grade 13, Jeannot was invited to an Ottawa Rough Riders high school camp to get an opportunity to show off his skills to American universities. He was offered a scholarship to play for Lenoir-Rhyne University in Hickory, North Carolina and showed up for football camp in mid-August of that year.

The experience at Lenoir-Rhyne was not a good one. From the beginning, it was obvious that the coaches did not have the same level of respect for players that Jeannot had become accustomed to in Canada. On top of that, the atmosphere in a southern college town in the 1960s did not reflect the morals and principles Jeannot had grown up embracing. The final straw came when the coaches would not let him enroll in the Economics classes he wanted because the class schedule conflicted with football practice. Jeannot returned to Ottawa after three weeks and enrolled in St. Patrick's College. In 1967, St. Patrick's College amalgamated with Carleton University, and Jeannot found himself playing for the Ravens. In '67, he caught a lot of passes from Al Morissette and should have been an all-star. The next year, Jeannot continued to be outstanding, this time with Mike Sharp throwing him passes. A gifted overall athlete, Jeannot had size and speed, making him hard to tackle after the catch.

Moe recalls that Jeannot decided to follow in his brother's footsteps and pursue a career in Physical Education. Since Carleton did not have a Physical Education program, Jeannot transferred to the University of Ottawa.

He sat out the 1970 season because of the transfer rule, although he participated on the practice squad for the Gee-Gees. Don Gilbert became the Gee-Gees head coach in 1971, and he brought in former Ottawa Rough Riders tight end Jay Roberts to work with Jeannot. Jeannot excelled as the Gee-Gees tight end and team captain for three years. Not only was he one of the most respected players in Canada, by opposing teams, but his charisma and natural wit endeared him to his teammates.

> He was always humble and interested more in others than himself.
> He loved games of all kinds—and was hard to beat when winning mattered!

Steve Carlo, one of Jeannot's teammates at Ottawa, recalls Jeannot's last game in the Yates Cup against Wilfred Laurier.

Our team had been decimated with injuries prior to the game against Laurier. We had lost half of our defensive line, two or three of our running backs, and we were down to our third string quarterback. Late in the game with the Gee-Gees trailing 42–0, a pass was thrown to Jeannot, requiring him to leap high in the air. The minute he caught the ball Larry Uteck drilled him in the back. He almost cut him in half, but Jeannot held on to the ball. When Jeannot returned to the huddle, one of his teammates said, "Nice catch, Jean." Jeannot just looked at him, with his piercing blue eyes, and nodded. That moment captured who Jeannot was to his teammates. 'Jean was John Wayne with a moustache.' He was our role model."

Jeannot was drafted by the Argonauts following the 1973 season. He competed against the six foot five inch 235 pound Peter Muller for the tight end position and was the last cut from the Argos in 1974. Jeannot returned to Ottawa, obtained his teacher's certificate, and started his career as a teacher.

An Educator and a Coach

Following graduation, Jeannot went to work as teacher at the J. S Woodworth Public School in Kingston, Ontario, and then went to work at A.J. Jackson Secondary with his brother Moe. He taught Physical Education and English. After three or four years, an opportunity came open at Colonel By Secondary School in Ottawa for a Physical Education teacher and guidance counselor. Jeannot took the job and spent the rest of his career at Colonel By.

Jeannot coached multiple sports but made his mark as the coach of the school's powerhouse rugby team. During his time as their coach, Jeannot took the team to Wales and to the Caribbean. He is remembered as an exceptional coach, teacher, and guidance counselor. One of the things that he was most proud of was establishing and coordinating a program for premier athletes at Colonel By. He retired in 2003.

A Competitor to the End

When asked about his special characteristics, Moe Rodrigue spoke of his brother's battle with kidney cancer and his refusal to give in.

Jeannot was first diagnosed with kidney cancer approximately 15 years ago. He had an operation to remove the infected kidney, but the cancer came back two years later. Jeannot was able to find a talented team of doctors and agreed to subject himself to experimental medicine. With the help of his doctors and his positive outlook, Jeannot was able to stretch the normal prognosis of five years to ten.

While he was fighting cancer, Jeannot was upbeat and positive and a pleasure to be around. He organized a breakfast club consisting of some of his former teammates and boys who had played for him. They met on Thursday mornings, and many of the attendees would join the group to be around Jeannot.

> It was a real tribute to him to see all his friends rally around him.

Bruce MacGregor recalls one of the last times he saw Jeannot:

> In 2012, there was a reunion of the Rideau teams which had won championships in '62 and '63. Jeannot was all set to attend, but right before the event, his cancer acted up, and he was unable to join us. Weeks later, we found out he was feeling better, so the six of us who had organized the reunion invited Jeannot to a special gathering at a restaurant in Ottawa South near his home. It was a great evening, and he was SO grateful that we had done this for him. He seemed like the picture of health as we laughed and reminisced for hours.
>
> He fought heroically, there were times when he couldn't get out of bed, but on Thursday morning he would find a way to get to breakfast with his friends. It was pretty special for his friends to see him the way he was, in good humor and with his positive outlook.

Sadly, Jeannot lost his battle with cancer on June 6, 2014. Bruce MacGregor recalls hearing of Jeannot's memorial service:

> I wasn't able to attend, but I heard it was absolutely packed—not surprising, as he was a wonderful guy, full of humor and warmth.

Brian Gervais #75

Dalhousie University – Offensive End
First Team All-Canadian – 1971

Brian was born in Niagara Falls, but his family moved to Sudbury when he was quite young. He played football for LaSalle Secondary and remembers that they had some good teams.

> We had a real solid football programme at LaSalle. We had some good coaches that got us started in the right direction.

Coach Rose

Brian had a lot of respect for head coach Harold Rose. He couldn't say enough good things about him:

> Harold had played football at Queens; he was a sharp young guy who built a good programme. He was really well liked by the whole student body, and the players loved him. To a lot of us guys, he was a father figure—a guy that we really looked up to and admired. Whatever he said was gospel. We'd run through a brick wall for him, so to speak. He really taught me a lot about how to approach the game from a mental standpoint. Coach Rose was just a good man; he really cared about his kids, and he always got the best out of us.

If I saw him on the street today, I would still call him Mr. Rose. I wouldn't call him by his first name even though we are friends. He's just one of those guys you respect.

Like many of the members of the 1971 All Canada Football Team, Brian feels that the impact a high school football coach has on the players they coach is immeasurable.

Especially in the early years, those kinds of men give you confidence in what you can accomplish and help you believe in yourself. They make you start dreaming. Yeah, we owe a lot to those guys.

The Hamilton Tiger Cat High School Camp

After football season in grade 12, Brian was invited to a high school camp sponsored by the Hamilton Tiger-Cats. He caught the eye of the Dalhousie University football coach, Dick Loiselle, and Dick offered him a scholarship to play football. Scholarships were not approved by the CIAU in 1970, but some schools were able to find money for tuition and other expenses to help some players get into the university:

> Being recruited by Dalhousie and having an opportunity to play football for the Tigers was a big help because we had grown up poor and didn't have much of a way to get to university.

In addition to earning a scholarship, Brian remembers his trip to the Hamilton Tiger Cat locker room for another reason:

> I was walking into the locker room where we had been told to report. I came to the door and opened it and suddenly realized there was something in front of me. That something was Angelo Mosca. I kept looking up until my neck was bent back, and I thought, 'Holy smoke! This guy is big.' I had never seen anybody as big as this guy. I said, 'Excuse me, Mr. Mosca,' and I stepped back and held the door for him.

By the way, Angelo Mosca was the six foot four inch 275 pound all pro tackle for the Hamilton Tiger-Cats.

The First Few Days of Married Life

Brian married his high school sweetheart right after high school, and they jumped on a train to take the 40-hour ride to Halifax. As he recalls, they "couldn't afford a sleeping car, so [they] sat up the whole way."

Upon arriving with their truckload of wedding gifts and $230, their first task was to find a place to stay. They walked from the train station to the university campus and found Coach Loiselle. He asked them where they were staying, and when they told him they had no place to stay, he put them up in his house for the next three days until they found an apartment.

Football and School at Dalhousie and the University of Western Ontario

Brian played for Dalhousie for four years and coached his fifth year while working on a degree in Physical Education. These years were not good years from a football perspective, other than in 1971 when he was selected to the All Canada Football Team.

> I think we won four games in the four years I played. I blew out my knee in the third game of the 1972 season, my draft year, so I missed the rest of the season, and, of course, did not get a look by the CFL.

Wanting an opportunity to play in the CFL and still having one year of eligibility left, Brian transferred to the University of Western Ontario where he hoped to get the exposure he needed to get a shot at the CFL. As it turned out, Brian had a good year and with the connections Coach Semotiuk had, he got the opportunity he was looking for. Brian was offered a contract to try out with the Ottawa Rough Riders.

"I Was a Slow White Guy."

> Getting into the CFL was awesome! Realistically, I never thought it would happen to me because I didn't think I was gifted enough physically. I was a smart player, and I was really versatile. I could do a lot of things. I had good skills, a good attitude, and I had had good coaching. So, I had a good background, but I was a slow white guy, trying to keep up with the best from Canada along with talented players from the U.S.
>
> I really trained hard and got in the best shape possible and just went in with a positive attitude. I thought, 'Hey! Go for it!'

Making It in the CFL

Ottawa had some very talented receivers, including Tony Gabriel and Jim Foley, which made it even more challenging. Brian remembers lining up in practice opposite a defensive back who had played for Notre Dame.

> I'm looking at this guy, and I'm thinking, 'Holy smoke! I'm trying to beat a guy who played for Notre Dame!'

The thing that amazed Brian at the professional level was how good the players were <u>and</u> how smart they were. The guys from the U.S. had been playing 10 or 12 games a year for 10 years or more. They knew how to play the game. "It was overwhelming," he said, "but I just went for it."

Brian made the team, and his first year's salary was $10,000, which he thought was all the money in the world. He started out on the taxi squad and made it into a few games that first year.

> Practice was just like a game to me. I was going to learn as much as I could from the vets. I just loved that I had a chance to go to practice with these guys and learn and grow as a player.

Three weeks before the end of the season, the Rough Riders had to make a roster change. Brian was cut as management did not think he would be picked up, but Calgary picked him up anyway. Ottawa won the Grey Cup that year, and Brian missed an opportunity to be a part of it.

Brian had two good years with the Stampeders as a starter, but after developing knee problems he was traded to Toronto. After a few weeks in Toronto, he was traded to Winnipeg where he played for two more years and finished his career.

Realizing a Dream

> I was able to accomplish far more than I ever thought possible. If I'd just been able to go to training camp, that would have been great. If I had just made the team and been on special teams my whole career, that would have been great. To become a starter...it was all bonus. It was awesome!

> I would have played in the CFL for nothing. If they had told me to get a job and that we would be practicing after work and playing on the weekends, I would have done it. I was built for the sport. I loved the physical contact and everything about it: the camaraderie, the teamwork. I am very thankful and grateful for the way things turned out.

Life Changing

Brian got much more out of his experience in the CFL than his salary and an opportunity to play pro football. Through exposure to Athletes in Action, Brian became a Christian and has spent the rest of his life involved in Christian ministry.

> I was your typical jock, typical university student, party guy. I wanted to have more fun than anybody else. I was also a real seeker, too, sort of a philosophical guy. I wanted to get answers to the big questions. Spiritually, I was looking for answers to a lot of questions, but for years I was looking for the exotic answers.

In Ottawa, there were three guys on the team: Jerry Orgon, Rod Woodward, and Wayne Tosh. They were Christians and through them Brian found out about the pregame chapel program put on by Athletes in Action. He was invited to attend one of the pregame programs, and things started to change.

> As I started to go to these meetings, I began seeing things I had been searching for my whole life. So, actually, I became a Christian during training camp. Then, through the ministry of Athletes in Action, I started to share my faith in Christ with young people in the cities where we lived, at different conferences, and wherever opportunities presented themselves. I actually worked on staff with Athletes in Action after I finished with the CFL, and with pro ministries in Vancouver, with the Lions, the Canucks, and a Triple-A baseball team. I did a lot of youth ministry and ran a Christian basketball league in Abbotsford, where I live now. I am now doing missionary work in China as well.

When Brian reflects on his life and the role that football played in it, he is convinced that it was part of God's plan for him.

> What you learn in football sticks with you your whole life. It makes you a better person, a better team player. It turns you into the kind of person that people can depend upon.

Reflections on His Football Career

When asked if he would have done anything differently, Brian jokingly responded by saying, "I probably should have played baseball or hockey." He went on to say he would have loved to have caught those passes he dropped.

He said that for years after his All-Canadian year, all he could think about were three passes he dropped that could have been touchdowns.

Why didn't I catch those? It would have been a perfect season.

Most guys that have athletic success are perfectionists by nature, but you have to keep that under control. Brian eventually reconciled his issues with the dropped passes and came to an insightful conclusion. He thought, "Hey, stupid. You were the best in the nation at your position. Be satisfied with that."

John Buda #66

University of Waterloo – Offensive Tackle
First Team All-Canadian 1971 and 1972

John was born in Toronto and played high school football for Runnymeade Collegiate in Toronto. Like many of the members of the 1971 CIS All Canada Football Team, John was a standout football player in high school. He was selected to the All Toronto team twice, and his senior year he was joined by two of his teammates. One of his high school teammates, Cor Doret, was also selected to the CIS All Canada Football Team with John in 1972.

Deciding on a University

John was heavily recruited by both Canadian and U.S. universities but remembers selecting the University of Waterloo because, as he said, "They wanted me." He recalls receiving recruiting letters from a number of universities, and some sent follow-up letters, but the University of Waterloo invited him to campus, and John remembers coaches from Waterloo making him feel pretty important.

When he arrived for his first year, John said he knew he was there to play football but was not sure what he wanted to study. He took "everything under the sun" but describes his course of studies as being very general that first year.

Adjusting to the College Game

John said it took him a couple of years to adjust to playing football at the university level. He was big for a high school player in Toronto, but in university everyone was just as big and just as strong. He found his first game playing for the University of Waterloo Warriors to be particularly intimidating.

> We played the University of Toronto at Varsity Stadium in front of 21,000 screaming fans. I had never played in front of so many spectators before.

He recalls that his first game was not a particularly good one, and the second game wasn't much better, adding, "It took me a few games to settle down."

John's second year at Waterloo was marked by injury.

> I missed three games because of a knee injury, and it really wasn't until my third year, 1971, that I started to play up to my potential. In 1971, I matured a lot, got stronger...and faster.

Realizing His Potential

John began to realize in 1971 that his speed and quickness were as big an asset to him as his size. He said that there were times when he was across the line before the defensive lineman had even moved.

> I wasn't stronger or heavier than a lot of my opponents, but I sure was quicker.

Like many of the members of the 1971 All Canada team, football was not his only sport. He wrestled for the University of Waterloo and came to realize that wrestling helped him develop his quickness, which was a big asset when he played football.

> Quick instant reactions helped me substantially. When you're playing against bigger people, you have to get on them quickly before they get those big bodies moving.

John reflected on the '71 season at Waterloo and expressed some frustration in the fact that they had not been as successful as they should have been. It was a disappointing season in his eyes.

> Our talent level was superior, but it did not result in us winning a lot of games.

He attributes some of their lack of success to the fact that they depended on the coaches to be the leaders rather than each other. "The guys have to lead," he said.

> I should have been more of a leader. I was looked up to because of my accomplishments, but I was a quiet guy. I needed to lead vocally, but I don't think I did. If I were playing today, I would not be quiet. I would have put every effort into being the leader the team needed. I know I could have done more. At Waterloo, I was never off the field. I played 60 minutes of every game. I just should have been more vocal.

John adds that they did turn the season around half way through, adding, "We lost our first three games, but we won our last three."

Moving Beyond the CFL

John had a shot at the CFL, but it was short-lived. He was drafted by the Toronto Argonauts and got into a couple of games with them, but as soon as some of the regulars got back off of injuries he was traded to Hamilton.

> I didn't even know I'd been traded. I showed up one day at practice, and the equipment manager asked me what I was doing there. I asked him what he meant by that, and his response was, 'You've been traded.'

John was in Hamilton for a short time and remembers it being a horrible place, and then he was traded to Calgary. He ended up in Calgary with three other players from Ontario: Wayne Dunkley from the University of Toronto, Paul Perras from McMaster University, and Paul Knill from the University of Western Ontario.

He recalls that none of the former CIS players liked the situation in Calgary. They didn't like the coach; they didn't like the culture, and they didn't appreciate being treated like second class citizens. They were all having dinner one night in Banff with another Canadian football player and John's girlfriend when they decided they'd had enough and should all quit the team. They all walked in the next day and turned their playbooks over to coach Jim Duncan. The next day the *Calgary Herald* carried the story of them quitting on its front page.

John coached a little high school football in the years right after he left the CFL, but to this day he does not follow the CFL or the NFL for that matter. He expressed frustration with the fact that it's difficult to find CIS sporting events on TV in Canada.

> The teams play good football, but we only see the playoff games and the Vanier Cup, and sometimes we can't even find those on TV.

Would You Do It Again?

When I asked John this he had a tough time answering right away.

> I had to think about this one a lot. I had a couple of injuries; we all did, but when I think of the guys I met, what football did for me, and what I did for football, the answer had to be yes. It's about the people you meet, and those special moments when you overcome adversity as a team—when you come together as a team. The last three games of the 1971 season, when we turned our season around, what a memory that was! During my first two-and-a-half years at Waterloo losing had become a habit. I started to think about how important it is to pick the right school. I thought I had chosen the wrong one.

John's Most Vivid Memories

> My most vivid memory of playing football at Waterloo was of the 1971 season. As I mentioned earlier, we turned our season around midway and won our last three games, including beating our archrival Waterloo Lutheran (now Wilfred Laurier University). We beat them handily, too.

John remembers a pivotal point in the season when the team was disappointed with their performance and decided to have a meeting at a local pub to discuss their season. Apparently, they indulged a little too much in the liquid refreshments, and some of the players took the post meeting activities a little too far. The next day, their coach, Wally Delahey, confronted the team. He told them that he had received a phone call from the president of the university, and that they had embarrassed the school with their activities the night before. Wally yelled at them for several minutes and then put them through the roughest two-and-a-half-hour workout they had ever experienced.

That incident was a turning point in their season. John doesn't know if it was the meeting they had or the fact that Wally had taken the blame for them, but from that point on the Warriors performed up to their potential.

When Wally Delahey retired in the early 90s, John had the honor of presenting him with an award. During the presentation ceremony, John told the story of the incident in 1971, which drew a smile from Wally.

Finding Out About the All Canada Selection

On November 20, 1971, John was having breakfast with a friend and waiting for a teammate to arrive, so they could all go to the College Bowl in Toronto. He picked up a newspaper and started to read an article highlighting the teams that would be playing. Included in the article were the names of the players selected to the 1971 CIS All Canada team. John said he was looking through the list of names to see if there was anybody he knew when he found his name. He was shocked. "My God, this is absolutely wonderful!"

Where Is He Now?

John graduated from Waterloo with a BA in Economics and Sociology. He had always had an interest in the business side of things as well as managing people. In the 1970s, schools were turning out more social workers than there were jobs, so John followed his passion into human resources and has spent his entire career in this field. He reflected on the impact that playing football had on his career:

What is winning in business? It is team work, working as a team, and leadership. All of those are take-aways from football.

John is currently living in Calgary with his wife Gail.

The End Comes Quick

Ole Hensrud #52

University of Manitoba – Offensive Guard
First Team All-Canadian – 1971

Ole Hensrud grew up in Kenora, Ontario. He was an all-around athlete in high school, playing football and hockey as well as running track and high jumping.

Following in His Brother's Footsteps

Ole had an older brother who played football for the Lakewood High School Mustangs, so when Ole entered high school, he naturally followed in his brother's footsteps. He loved football but was also an outstanding hockey player.

> I had an opportunity to play hockey for a university in Minnesota on a hockey scholarship, but I decided to stick with football. I loved both sports.

Ole was a halfback in high school and led the Mustangs to the Northwestern Ontario football championship during one of the years he played for them. When he graduated from high school, he had an opportunity to play football for both Simon Fraser University and the University of Waterloo. As many of his buddies were headed toward southern Ontario, Ole decided to enroll at Waterloo to be closer to his teammates.

Adjusting to the College Game

When he started playing for Waterloo, he was moved from the backfield to the line. His first year he weighed 180 pounds, and at six feet tall he was by no means the biggest player on the team. He has vivid memories of this first game as a Warrior:

> They had moved me to tight end, and in our first game against Queens I lined up across from a six foot four inch 235 pound defensive end who was in his fifth year. Oh, what a learning experience that was! I didn't know what hit me.

After that first football season in Waterloo, Ole got homesick and decided to transfer to the University of Manitoba. Winnipeg was much closer to home, being two hours from Kenora instead of 19. It turned out to be an outstanding decision given the success the Bisons would experience in the next two years.

A Remarkable Experience Playing for the Bisons

Playing for Henry Janzen and the University of Manitoba Bisons for three years was a rewarding experience. Ole attributes their success to having a great bunch of team oriented guys as well as premiere coaching from Henry Janzen, Ray Ash, and the rest of the coaching staff.

> We had a small team. I never weighed more than 190 pounds, and I played on the offensive line. We were small, but we were fast. We learned to get off the line quickly an open a hole, so our backs would burst through. We just had to open a hole for a split second, and Hrycaiko or Shylo were through and into the opponent's backfield. Both Henry Janzen and Ray Ash were former Blue Bombers. Ray, our line coach, was less than six feet tall and had played guard in the CFL, so he knew how to coach a smaller line. I remember playing against Queens in the Western final. They probably outweighed us by ten to fifteen pounds per man.

Ole recalls that they never had too many fans at their games. "If we got 300 or 400 at the stadium in Manitoba, that would be great. We were just playing for each other."

The First College Bowl

In 1969, the Bisons defeated the Windsor Lancers in the Churchill Bowl and advanced to play McGill University in the Vanier Cup at Toronto's Varsity Stadium. A lot of the players on his team were from the north end of Winnipeg, which was one of the poorer areas of town.

> We went down to Toronto, and there was a big dinner and awards presentation. A lot of the guys had to borrow sports jackets because they couldn't afford to buy them. After all, most of them never had to wear one before.

The sports writers didn't think we had a chance against McGill because we were such a small team. We won by a score of 24–15 and surprised everyone with our dedication and our play.

Competing in the West and Winning Again in 1970

Ole attributes their success in the playoffs to the competition in Western Canada.

> The football back then was tough. Calgary, Edmonton, and Saskatchewan were all made up of a bunch of farm boys. They were hard hitting and played hard-nosed football. You had to be tough to play against those big guys. When we went to play the eastern teams, it seemed like they didn't hit as hard. We were able to compete because of our speed, and, of course, we had Bob Kraemer, who was a great quarterback.

Ole felt he was a much more confident player in his last two years of football than he was in his first two.

> In the first two years, I didn't really know what was happening or what to expect. But later, I knew what to anticipate, and I was much quicker as a result. The experience made a big difference; it made everything so much easier.

In 1970, the Bisons won a hard-fought game against Queens in the Churchill Bowl. They eked out a 24–20 victory in overtime. Their second trip to the Vanier Cup resulted in at 38–11 victory over the Ottawa Gee-Gees.

Playing for Henry Janzen

Ole spoke fondly of coach Henry Janzen and the team culture he created at the University of Manitoba:

> We had a lot of good players and a lot of good times together. We had fun. We didn't have a lot of stars, but we played as a team, and no one was better than anyone else. And one of the greatest things about our coaches was that they never yelled at anyone. I've watched opposing teams and seen coaches tear into players who made mistakes. They yell and scream at the players, and then they bench them. Henry Janzen and his coaching staff were just the opposite. They never screamed at us once. They took us aside and talked to us. It was the kind of encouragement and reinforcement that you carry throughout your life.

Ole also liked the fact that everyone had to earn their spot on Janzen's team. It didn't matter how long you had played, if you didn't do your job you were pulled:

> If you made a mistake, they wouldn't pull you right away because they knew you would try twice as hard on the next play. But if you made the same mistake a second time, they pulled you right out. Someone else would go in, and if that person did a good job and played his heart out, you would have a tough time getting back in.

> When you played, you put yours whole self into it—your heart and your soul. You played for the team. I think that's what makes a winning team. They don't have a lot of heroes, but if they have a few, they're part of the team.

Concussions and Not Doing It Over Again

Like a lot of players, Ole didn't make it through his four years of college football without a few concussions:

> I got dinged a couple of times. Each time I got back up, went back to the huddle, and someone told me where to go for the next few plays. In the 'old days,' you didn't come out of the game. One time I got kicked in the head, and I was out of it. But the guys told me what to do until we turned the ball over, and then I came out of the game.

Ole is sure that those concussions and other football injuries have caught up with him. As a result, he doesn't think he would go through it all again.

Life After Football

Upon completing his degree in Physical Education, Ole returned to Kenora and joined his father in the bricklaying trade. He coached football at the local high school for a couple of years, and in the early 1980s had an opportunity to take his skills to the west coast and start working in heavy industry. He became a refractory bricklayer and started building refineries, pulp mills, glass plants, and even crematoriums. His work took him all across Canada, from one coast to the other.

Ole feels that the lessons he learned on the football field served him well in his career:

> It's all teamwork. You get a crew because you have a job to do, and you've got to get them together as a team. You set out a plan and a procedure, and you execute accordingly—just like in football. If you have a weak player, something has to be done.

Where Is He Now?

Ole has two children, a boy and a girl. His son is a fireman in Vancouver, and his daughter is a nurse. His son played baseball and soccer and still plays soccer in his spare time. Ole's daughter was a dancer. She has her CMA and works for Lotto BC.

At the time of this writing, Ole is awaiting the arrival of his first grandchildren. His daughter is expecting twins in July! Needless to say, Ole and his wife, Diane, are quite excited about the idea of being grandparents.

The End Comes Quick

Cam Innes #40

University of Windsor – Center
First Team All-Canadian – 1971

Cam Innes was born in Windsor, Ontario, which he describes as a great sports town, heavily influenced by its close proximity to the U.S. Windsor had a great sports system.

Beginning a Career in Windsor

Cam started playing peewee football when he was 12 years old. He ended up at Walkerville High School in Windsor where he participated in multiple sports:

> I was involved in all kinds of sports in addition to football. I played basketball; I curled and was even a high jumper (a long time ago). My family was actively involved in sports, and my two sisters and brother were athletes as well. Mom and Dad really supported us in our sports activities.

Cam recalls that one of his family members, Ian Allison, was the athletic director at Walkerville High School. Ian did not show any favoritism toward Cam even though they were related:

> He made sure I didn't get off the beaten path. He used to carry a stick and would whack me with it on occasion and tell me it was for the next time I got in trouble.

Cam had great high school coaches and as a result was able to play on a couple of championship teams. Walkerville won a championship in football and also in basketball, where Cam was the sixth man on the team.

Moving on to Play for Queens

Cam's dad was a Queens graduate, and although Cam visited with John Metras at Western, he was destined to play football for Queens. On a campus visit with his father, Cam says, "He took me to the med school, the engineering school, and the Physical Education school. I broke his heart when I decided to enroll in Phys. Ed., but then I ended up working with engineers for the better part of my career."

Cam played for Queens in 1968 when they won the national championship, and he was a co-captain when they lost to Manitoba in the Western Bowl in 1970. He was selected to the all-conference team in 1970, and Edmonton selected him in the first round of the 1971 draft.

He recalls what a great experience it was playing for Queens and Frank Tindall, their legendary long-term coach:

> I observed him when he was working, and I thought, 'jeez, that guy is having a ball,' and it influenced me to become a college football coach. I thought to myself, 'That would be a great job.'

The University of Windsor and the CFL

Edmonton offered Cam $6,500 to play for them in 1971, but he'd also been granted a scholarship to start his master's degree in sports management at the University of Windsor. He chose to pursue his master's degree and to play another year of college football.

> I played for Gino Fracas, another Hall of Fame guy, at Windsor in 1971 when I was working on my master's. In the course of events, my CFL rights were traded to Montreal, and they offered me $3,000 more than I had been offered the year before. I had my master's degree under my belt, except for my dissertation, so I thought I'd give the CFL a try.

Cam tried out with the Als in the summer of 1972. Larry Smith was on that team as a rookie as well. Larry stuck it out with the Als, and Cam opted to accept a coaching job at St. Francis Xavier to work as an assistant to Don Loney. He moved down to the Maritimes in the fall of 1973. Little did he know what lay ahead of him.

A Dream Come True

Cam remembers the day he was called into Don Loney's office to receive the news of his promotion to head coach.

> I had finished my dissertation and my master's, so I took the opportunity to become the assistant coach. Eight months later, I was appointed head coach because Don retired. Here I was...26 years old...and I had my lifelong dream.

As Don outlined his retirement and informed Cam of his appointment, what happened next was permanently etched in his memory:

> I remember leaving Don's office, and I went to center field of Oland Field. I looked skyward and said, 'Dear Lord, help me because I have no idea what I have gotten myself into.'

Cam spent four years at StFX. The first two were rebuilding years, but before he left he took the team to the playoffs and earned a couple of 'coach of the year' awards. "I spent a ton of time away from home recruiting in Ontario and Quebec and also in New England. Twenty-five percent of our players were from the States."

Moving on to Ottawa

After some time had passed, Cam was beginning to think that he needed to get into "mainstream" football in Canada, so when the head football coaching job came open at the University of Ottawa in 1978, he moved on it. He joined them in May of 1978.

The Ottawa Gee-Gees had won the Vanier Cup in 1975, but after that they brought in a couple of part-time high school coaches to run the program. Of course, without full-time coaching, the program faltered. Cam was hired as the first full-time football coach, but to justify the position, he was also assigned to be the assistant basketball coach. This was indicative of Canadian physical education at the time—you simply did everything. As Cam says, "They got the most out of you for their $10,000."

Once again in another rebuilding situation, Cam found some great coaches and started recruiting hard.

> We got really lucky. I was a good recruiter and was able to bring in some great talent, including Rick Zmich, who was a great quarterback and ultimately the Hec Crighton Award winner. In 1980, we took the team to the Vanier Cup against the University of Alberta. I was selected as the coach of the year that year. I also served two years as the president of the football association in Canada.

Moving on and a Change in Careers

Following the 1980 season, Cam began to question the University of Ottawa's long-term commitment to sustaining a winning football program. He decided it was time for a change, so he applied for and was accepted into the University of Western's MBA program. Although he coached a little during training camp, the demands of the MBA program kept him off the field.

During this time, Cam received a call from the University of Calgary, offering him an opportunity to become the first marketing director for athletics in Canada. He would have to help coach football as well, but it sounded like a great opportunity and gave him the chance to coach with Peter Connellan and resulted in one more trip to the Vanier Cup.

> Not only was I able to set up the marketing program, but the Calgary Dinos ended up winning the national championship in 1983.

After that season, Cam returned to Western and finished his MBA in 1985. Another phone call took him back to Calgary, this time as the marketing and public relations director for the Calgary Stampeders, a job he held for two years.

In 1988, Cam traded football helmets and shoulder pads for hard hats and coveralls as he began using his coaching skills to help workers in the oil and gas business, primarily drilling and completions. This phase of his career lasted 27 years until his retirement in January 2016. The career resulted in a relocation from Calgary to Houston, Texas, where he now enjoys mild winters and the best high school football in North America.

Football Values

Cam spoke fondly of the values he learned from Frank Tindall, Gino Fracas, and Peter Connellan: those being character, teamwork, and purpose.

> These are the values I took away from football. The coaches that I named are the type of individuals that I would want my son to be coached by. I wouldn't mind being in that category myself.

Cam frequently used his football stories to help communicate his lessons to the men he was working with in the oil field. He found that they not only helped convey his message, but they kept the men's interest up as well.

> I have had some rewarding times both in the oil patch and in football. I look back on that with a great deal of pride.

Fondest Memories

When asked, Cam identified the following as his fondest football memories:

- The 1968 National Championship at Queens
- Being selected co-captain of the team at Queens in 1970 with Jim McKeen
- Being selected co-captain at Windsor with Ross McDonald in 1971
- Receiving the Frank Tindall Trophy as National Coach of the Year in 1980

> Recognition by your peers is really special, especially looking back on it. I was very fortunate that we got together with some great guys and great teams and great efforts. It's the application of the purpose part of it, working together as a team, that really cemented that value.

Keith Johnston #55
Mcmaster University – Offensive Guard
First Team All-Canadian – 1971

Shifting gears to talk about myself feels odd, since that wasn't my intent when beginning the journey that has become this book, but I'll try my best to share **my experiences** and what they meant to me. My first recollection of football was watching Joe Kapp, the quarterback for the Calgary Stampeders, play in Mewata Stadium in Calgary. I played sandlot football with my friends from 22A street in Calgary, which was less than a mile from where McMahon Stadium would be erected in 1960, the year my family moved to Dallas, Texas.

Good Coaching at an Early Age

I started playing organized football in grade seven. The coach put me on the line, which is where new kids usually end up. There were only 13 players on the team, so I played both offensive and defensive tackle.

My real break came the next year when I had an opportunity to try out for the varsity team at T.C. Marsh Junior High in Dallas. As it was the first year for the school, the coaches were allowed to start two-a-day practices early, and they invited every eighth and ninth grade football player to try out.

There were probably 80 boys trying out for 36 spots. The head coach was Roland Hallmark, and the offensive line coach was Howard Evans. The two coaches had been teammates at the University of Houston and both were early in their coaching careers.

I didn't think I had much of a chance to make the team as I was only five foot two inches and 110 pounds. The next smallest lineman weighed 145 pounds. Fortunately, Coach Evans saw something in me he liked, and I ended up being one of four grade eight players to make the team.

While I didn't play much that first year, I did start in a couple of games and played enough to earn a letter and gain valuable experience. Little did I know I'd play for Coaches Hallmark and Evans for another four years. In 1964, W.T. White High School was built, and the coaching staff from T.C. Marsh moved to the new high school.

Struggling in a New School

Playing football for a new school in Dallas wasn't easy. The first year, we only had grades ten and eleven. Fortunately, we weren't forced to play a varsity schedule. We played new schools like us, a few JV teams, and a couple of varsity teams from smaller schools. I think we won two games the first year, and one game the second.

I started at offensive guard all three years in high school and even had a chance to play some defense. Three years playing for arguably the best line coach in Dallas helped me develop skills that would pay off when I moved up to college football.

Howard Evans started for the University of Houston for three years at center and middle linebacker and was all-conference two of those years. He was five foot eleven inches tall and a little over 200 pounds, so he knew how to coach smaller linemen. Where Howard helped develop our skills, Roland Hallmark taught us to be passionate about the game and to take pride in how we played.

Coach Hallmark had a lot of confidence in me and said if I weighed 175 pounds I had a good chance of being selected to the All-City team. Unfortunately, I missed the last three games of my junior year with a dislocated elbow, and as a result of a bad case of bronchitis, showed up for fall practice my senior year weighing only 150 pounds.

I thought I would spend the summer before my senior year living on my uncle's farm in Saskatchewan, eating three huge meals a day, and coming back at 175. Unfortunately, I lost 10 pounds instead.

Deciding on a College Was Easy

Given my size, and a less than stellar senior year, I had few options for playing college football. My best friend, David Goodney, was planning on attending Austin College in Sherman, Texas. Sherman was only 60 miles north of Dallas, and given they did not award athletic scholarships, my chances of playing some football were much greater.

Austin had a good football program but was primarily known for its academics. My friend David was one of the smartest kids in my high school and was a pretty good football player. He chose Austin College for the academics, but we both decided to try out for the football team.

I visited Austin College with David and three of my high school teammates. Coach Floyd Gass was really interested in my teammates as all of them had been recognized as first or second team All-City in Dallas. At the end of our day on campus, he sat us all down and told each of us how we could contribute to the team our first year. By the time he got to me, he couldn't remember what position I played. When I told him I was a guard, he said, "Oh yeah? We need those, too." Austin College was a much more expensive school than the state schools, so going there was going to put a financial strain on my parents. I was able to secure a small amount of financial aid, and since my dad really wanted to see me play college football, he managed to find the money for me.

My Dad, My Inspiration

My dad had been an all-around athlete at Vaughn Road Collegiate in Toronto in the 1930s. He played all sports, including football, track, lacrosse, and especially baseball. He loved sports and loved to watch me and my brother Ron compete.

I think Mom and Dad attended every one of my games when I was playing in high school and every home game when I played for Austin College. They also came to a few away games. Dad surprised me a couple times, once showing up in Nebraska in 1969, and he and Mom surprised me in Windsor when I was playing for McMaster. I looked up in the stands for my dad after every TD we scored, and we signaled to each other.

Austin College – Highs and Lows

I broke into the starting lineup at Austin College (AC) three games into my freshman season and held onto that starting role for my entire four-year career. Winning came easier for AC than it did in high school; in fact, in 1968, the Kangaroos finished the season sixth in the nation, having won eight of their nine games.

> 1968 was an amazing season. It was a thrill to play for such a strong team. Unfortunately, our head coach, Floyd Gass, catapulted into Division I and became the head coach at Oklahoma State University after our 1968 season. He took most of his coaching staff with him, so AC dropped to 7–2 in 1969 and a dismal 3–6 in my final season.

Although the team struggled in 1970, it was one of my better years. My teammates made me a co-captain, and I was selected to the All Texas College team.

Moving to Canada for an MBA and an Extra Year of Football

While I earned a BA in Economics from AC, I wasn't quite sure what to do with it, so I started looking into graduate school. My aunt, Sadie Ludlow, (the administrative assistant to McMaster University's president) suggested that I check out McMaster's MBA program. When I found out I was eligible to play football for the Marauders, I applied for the MBA program, packed my bags, and headed for Hamilton.

> Playing football for McMaster was like a dream come true. I wasn't sure how I would be accepted by the Mac players, or if I could even make the team, since the team was much bigger than what I was used to at AC. It wasn't the first time I had to compete against bigger players, but I decided a few pounds couldn't hurt. I gained 11 and showed up for training camp weighing 196.

Thankfully, the Marauder football team accepted me, and I quickly earned the nickname "Tex," which was a little ironic given I was the shortest lineman at five-feet, nine-inches tall. I earned a starting position on the offensive line, and for the first time in my football career, I played on a team that competed in the playoffs.

Playing for Mac was one of my most enjoyable years as a player. My teammates were fantastic, and I enjoyed playing for Coach Ray Johnson and Sam Scoccia. The All-Canadian selection was icing on the cake and was totally unexpected.

Lessons Learned

The most valuable lesson I took away from my years in football is that success is the result of teamwork and collaboration. Teamwork grows when there is trust, and trust is developed in the day-to-day interactions on the practice field.

A Career in Business and Football

During my second year, I helped coach the Mac line, but after graduation I returned to Texas and started my career as a consultant with Arthur Andersen. I spent the next 30 years helping companies in the oil and gas industry develop systems to manage their businesses. For the past 15 years, I've worked as an independent consultant, helping people develop leadership skills. While most of my career was spent in Houston, I also worked in Calgary and London, England.

A few years in, I became interested in officiating football. I wanted to stay close to the game. Officiating allowed me to have a career and be actively involved in the game I love. I spent 27 years officiating high school football in Texas.

> I tell people that football is in my blood. I've spent more than 50 years on a football field, between playing, officiating, and in the last few years, photographing and coaching football in Vernon, BC. One of my biggest thrills was being on the field in Vancouver photographing the Vanier Cup when McMaster won its first Vanier Cup in 2011.

Wondering If I Would You Do It Again

When I spoke with all the other guys, this question was always one that came up because there is hardly a day that goes by that I don't long to put on the pads one more time.

When I was coaching high school football a few years ago, I occasionally put on a helmet and got into my stance to show the boys how it's done. I even tried to take some of them on without a helmet one day. I hate to think what would have happened if they had taken me up on my challenge. After that experience, I encouraged the players to tell me to 'act my age' if I tried to do that again.

One day in practice, I demonstrated a blocking technique that involved running through a blocking dummy and rolling on the ground on the other side. As I picked myself up off the ground, I heard one of the players say: "My grandfather couldn't do that."

I can't imagine what my life would have been like had I not played football. The game has blessed me every step of the way.

My closest friends are my former teammates. I now have twenty new friends as a result of this project.

Where You Can Find Me Now

I currently live in Vernon, BC with my wife Sylvia. I am actively involved in Rotary activities, which includes chairing the Rotary Athletic Awards; an annual event which I initiated to recognize high school athletes in our area. My daughter Caitlin lives in Boston, Massachusetts.

Wayne Conrad #55

University of Calgary – Offensive Tackle
First Team All-Canadian – 1971

Wayne Conrad took one of the most unusual routes to his year at the University of Calgary and six years with the Montreal Alouettes. But there is nothing usual about Wayne, other than his passion for the game of football and the degree to which he attributes his success in life and business to it.

The Knothole Gang in Edmonton

Wayne says that he grew up in Edmonton, spending his time outside of Clarke Stadium as a member of the "knothole gang," adding, "We would play with whatever we could to simulate the game of football."

Wayne quickly graduated to playing bantam football and was a quarterback in the early years. He remembers winning the provincial championship a couple of times and, as co-captain of the team, receiving the trophy from Jackie Parker.

> They took our picture for the paper. Ian MacLeod was my co-captain. I remember that picture because I had my fly down! I was 12 years old and that started my career off with a bang.

An Early Introduction to Professional Football

Wayne moved to Calgary while still in his early teens and began playing junior football for the Mount Royal College Cougars when he was 16 years old.

I was a linebacker then. Most of the players on the team were 18–21 years old. I had my first tryout with the Calgary Stampeders when I was just 17. My contract was for $4,200. I was cut from the Stampeders twice, and the BC Lions twice, but I did end up playing for the Victoria Steelers in the Continental League. The Continental League was where the CFL and NFL stashed their cuts in the 1960s.

Wayne played for Coach Don McKeta, the head coach of the Victoria Steelers and received " $14 a week…and all the bruises [he] could take."

Wayne recalls that Coach McKeta had been rated in *Sports Illustrated* as one of the 10 meanest coaches in college football when he was coaching for the University of Washington. Wayne's first experience with him confirmed that rating. In his first practice, he was told to go one-on-one for 30 minutes with every other lineman on the team. The confrontation with Coach McKeta at the conclusion of that 30-minute drill still stands out in Wayne's mind:

> I broke down and started crying, then I told him, 'I'm going to go to the can over here, then I'm going to come back and kick your ass all over this field.' McKeta turned to me and said, 'Wayne, you've made the team.'

Enrolling and Playing for the University of Calgary

After the 1969 season, and another cut from the CFL, Wayne decided it was time to forget about football and get an education. Getting into university was going to be a challenge as Wayne had only completed grade 9 and a couple of months in high school:

> I was a bit of a rogue, and the only book I had read up until then was *The Adventures of Huckleberry Finn*.

He met with Dennis Kadatz, the director of athletics at the University of Calgary, who told him that if he agreed to play football he would be allowed into the "adult program," but he would be ineligible his first year because he had played "professional" football with Victoria. Wayne agreed to sit out the 1970 season and enrolled in the adult program.

Wayne played offensive guard for the Dinos and Coach Mike Lashuk during the 1971 season and was selected to the All-Canadian team at the end of the season. He was described by Max Abraham, the three time All-Canadian for Saskatchewan, as "the best lineman I ever played against."

Wayne recalls being in a bar when he found out he had been selected All-Canadian...but he wasn't drinking. He was working! He spent many years working as a bouncer in bars in Calgary and claims many of his body parts have been shot at and cut.

Moving on to a Career with the Alouettes

At the conclusion of the 1971 football season, Wayne received a call from J.I. Albrecht with the Montreal Alouettes, informing him that they had acquired his rights from the BC Lions and wanted him to come to their training camp. Given his track record with the CFL, Wayne wanted to make sure he would get something out of this next experience, so he insisted that he get something "up front" for agreeing to sign a contract.

> Albrecht said, 'I'll give you a $10,000 contract with a $1,000 signing bonus.' I was so excited that I jumped in my car...and smashed into something. It cost me $300 to get my car repaired.

> Having negotiated a signing bonus, I decided to push my luck and told Albrecht that I wasn't going to show up at camp and find myself sixth on the depth chart. I got my wish. I was listed as fifth my first day.

> I went into camp as a guard, but on a day when the two centers both missed the same practice, Sam Etchevery asked if anyone could play center. I immediately said that I could, but I would have also told him the same thing if he had asked for a quarterback.

Having never played center before, Wayne found the adjustment to having to make a long snap particularly intimidating.

> Before each game, I would be petrified about having to long snap. You could put a 300 pound guy in front of me, and it wouldn't bother me a bit, but I hated those 3rd down snaps. The guys fielding the snaps would have to be either good shortstops or NBA players.

Wayne recalls snapping the ball over the head of the Al's punter, Wally Buono, in a playoff game during his first season.

> We lost the game and got knocked out of the playoffs. I thought my career was over...then I got a call from Marv Levy. Marv told me that the line coach had graded me out as one of his top linemen.

When you look up Wayne Conrad's name in the CFL history books, you'll find a lot about his accomplishments, but what you won't see is that Wayne, at five foot eleven inches and 220 pounds, was the smallest center to play in the CFL since 1947.

What Football Meant to Wayne

It's clear that football played a huge role in shaping Wayne's life; in fact, Wayne claims that if it wasn't for football he would not be here today.

> Football saved my life. Without it, I might've ended up in the penitentiary. Basically, I was a street kid. I was hard to handle. I've done a lot of different things, including bringing a submarine from Russia to Vancouver.

When I probed him further about that submarine, he described acquiring and transporting a Russian sub from Vladivostok in the Soviet Union to Vancouver as being more rewarding than winning a Grey Cup. There was no way to capture the full impact of that story, so you'll just have to ask Wayne, but it was easy to for him to concisely convey what football has meant to him:

> I owe any success I have had in business to football, particularly being unafraid of failure. If you've got a fear of failure you're doomed, especially in the business world.

Wayne claims that football taught him how to survive, be competitive, chase his passion, and be successful. He believes that if you want to be successful you have to know how to fight through difficulties:

> If you want to succeed, you'll give it all that you have, and then your body and soul will tell you, 'You've done the very best you can.' That's when you can look in the mirror and say, 'Okay.'

Philosophy on Winning

Football had such a huge impact on Wayne's life that he's thought about the sport and its meaning on many occasions. He shared his philosophy on winning:

> If you haven't lost, you really don't know how to win. You have to lose to know what it takes to win.

"I Would Not Have Played Football"

When asked if he would do anything differently if he had it all to do over again, Wayne shared the same sentiments as Larry Smith and Brian Gervais. All three men played for several years in the CFL, and all three questioned whether the toll the professional game took on their bodies was worth it.

> I played six years at a higher level, the pros. Guys there are bigger and faster. Everybody is going 100 miles per hour, and you think to yourself, 'Holy Christ! This is really fast.' You add the extra six years on your body, and then you get to be 70 years old. The price you pay later in life to play that sport, which is a violent, violent sport...physically, it's not worth it.

But he did clarify that statement in a way that resonates for many, if not all, of us: "Would I trade the friendships and the lessons and the discipline and the ability to overcome adversity? NEVER!"

A Heart as Big as the Game

Football meant a lot to Wayne, but like most football players, the most important part of the game was the friendships he developed. If you look up Wayne Conrad in Wikipedia, you will find the following:

> Wayne Conrad was a center / guard out of the University of Calgary. Conrad played six seasons for the Montreal Alouettes from 1972 to 1977. He won both an East and a CFL All-Star selection at center in 1975. Conrad played in three Grey Cup games with Montreal, losing once in 1975 and winning twice in 1974 and 1977. One of Conrad's

teammates from the 1977 Grey Cup season was defensive back Tony Proudfoot. When Proudfoot came down with ALS [also known as Lou Gehrig's Disease], Conrad auctioned off his jersey and Grey Cup ring to raise money for ALS. The following is a short article taken from the Saskatoon Star Phoenix in 2008.

Wayne Conrad, a centre on the Alouettes' 1977 championship team, is auctioning off his Grey Cup jersey and ring to raise funds for the ALS Society of Quebec and BC. "There's nothing you can do that's more sacred," Conrad told the Montreal Gazette's Herb Zurkowsky. "To be honest, I cherish it. I believe I have given the thing I cherish most. Do I love Tony Proudfoot? Yes, I do. Do I love his family? Yes, I do. Tony gave me that gift by calling me his friend." Money from a Vancouver fundraiser will also go to the Tony Proudfoot Fund. Proudfoot, a good friend and former teammate of Conrad's, suffers from ALS (Lou Gehrig's Disease).

Bob Mincarelli

Glenn Ponomarenko

Cam Innes

John Danaher

Wayne Dunkley

Bob Eccles

Keith Johnston John Buda

Wayne Dunkley

G. Ponomarenko

Brian Gervais

Chris Harber

Denny Hrycaiko

Dan Dulmage

Rick Chevers

Larry Smith

Carleton at Ottawa

THE END COMES QUICK

George Hill

Max Abraham

Bruce MacRae

Larry Smith

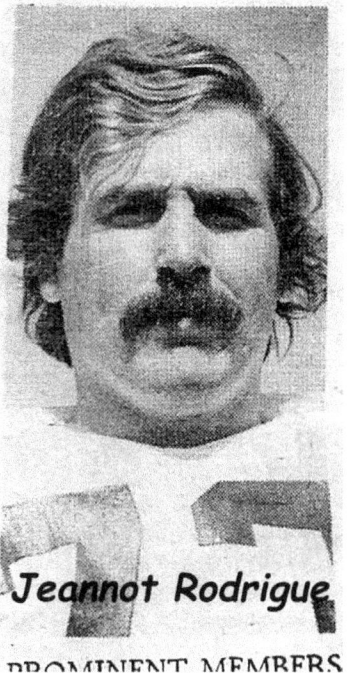

Jeannot Rodrigue

PROMINENT MEMBERS

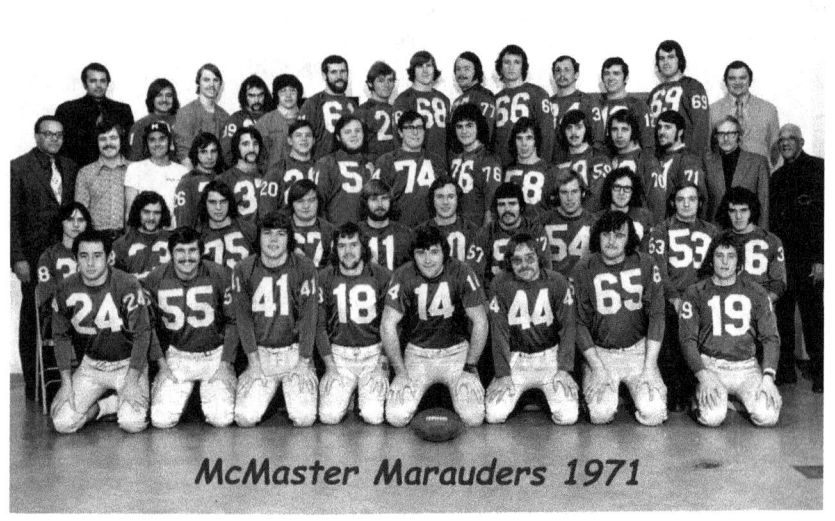

McMaster Marauders 1971

Barrie Reid   Keith Johnston   Max Abraham

Western vs Windsor

Western vs Ottawa

Bruce MacRae - Western

Wayne Conrad

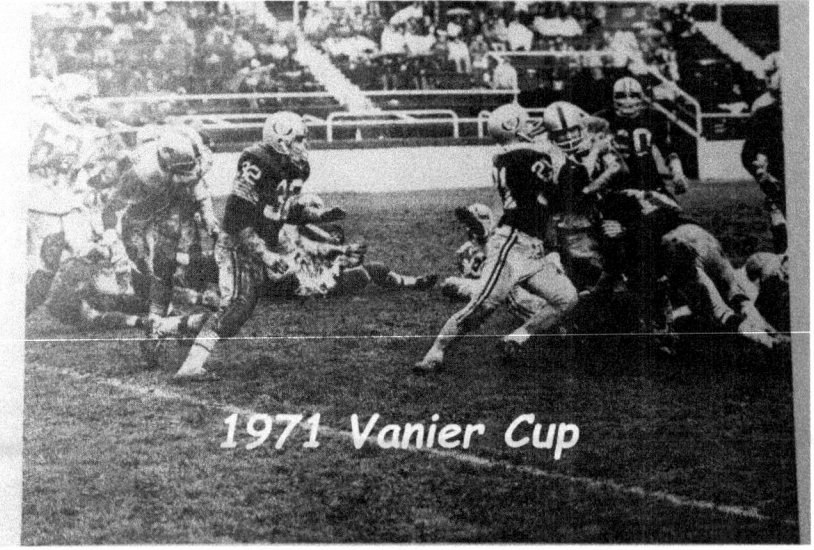
1971 Vanier Cup

The End Comes Quick

Dennis Hrycaiko

Western at McMaster 1971

The final play of the game as Ken Bauz (76) splits the uprights as Western defender Jim Karn (23) moves in attempting to block it.

Dan Dulmage #63

University of Western Ontario – Defensive End
First Team All-Canadian – 1971 and 1972

Dan grew up in Picton, Ontario, which is a small community south of Belleville. He attended Prince Edward Collegiate Institute, but the school did not have a football team until Dan's senior year:

> An old McGill alumnus organized a team. We were competitive but didn't win many games. We were rough old farm boys.

Dan's coach took him to meet Tom Mooney at McGill University, and Tom recruited Dan to play for the McGill Redmen.

Adjusting to College Football

Dan recalls what an adjustment it was in his first football training camp at McGill:

> It was a rude awakening from what I was used to at good ole PECI, with two-a-day practices. The team we ended up with was a mixture of oldies that were as old as the coaches and young guys like me. I was pretty green when I started out, but I gradually got into it. I took a lot of beatings.

Dan suffered a broken hand and also contracted a staph infection in his knee from the dirty laundry and getting run down. The team doctor swears he never said it, but they came close to removing his leg.

Dan made it through his first year and remembers how Coach Mooney found him a job for the next summer.

Tom took me into his office and showed me a map with a bunch of flags on it. He pointed at a flag and said, 'This is where you're going to work this summer.' It was Milhaven, where they were building a penitentiary. We worked like dogs all summer, and the training table was a beer at the Pickerton hotel.

The 1969 College Bowl

Dan put on 25 pounds that summer, which enabled him to pick up his game the next year. The 1969 season was a good year for the Redmen. They made it all the way to the College Bowl but lost to Manitoba by a score of 24–15. Unfortunately, Dan did not play in that game:

> We had played U of T in the final game of the season and beat them. In the post game celebration, even though Tom Mooney had a rule against drinking during the season, a few of the boys would have drinks now and then. After the game, we wandered over to where the fraternity houses were and ran into a few guys that didn't belong there. We were trying to get them out of the fraternity house when I got punched in the jaw. That punch cracked my jaw.

Dan thought he would still be able to play even though his jaw was wired up, but Coach Mooney had other ideas and said, "No. You played your cards, and you lost."

To add insult to injury, Coach Mooney sat their starting quarterback on the bench the week before the College Bowl game as the result of a disagreement between the two men during a media interview prior to leaving campus for the game in Toronto. The quarterback was George Wall, who Dan characterized as a good leader and an experienced quarterback. With Wall riding the bench, a rookie quarterback named Dan Smith from Ottawa started the game in George's place.

Finishing at McGill and Moving on to Western

During Dan's last year at McGill, the team was supposed to be a powerhouse. Dan was told he would be moved to offense when a six foot ten inch 340 pound defensive tackle showed up who had been playing for the West Virginia Volunteers. To quote Dan, "He was just enormous."

As it turned out, the big guy was out of shape and lasted less than a week:

> When he quit the team, I got his shoulder pads...which came down to my navel. I also got the big guy's jersey, but when I tucked it in, you could only see half the numbers. They moved me back to the defensive line.

Dan said that his line coach at McGill was Charlie Bailey, who had played in the CFL. The defensive coordinator was a former CFLer named George Alevausatos. Dan remembers that he was about five-foot, nine-inches tall and 250 pounds and could run as fast backwards as the linemen could run forward.

Sadly, the Redmen didn't live up to expectations in 1970, and at the end of the season, they announced that they were going to move into the Quebec league. With that, Dan and one of his teammates, Dave Doherty, decided to transfer to the University of Western Ontario. Dan had been accepted into their dental school and liked the fact that the dean of the dental school, Wes Dunn, was a big football fan. This proved to be a big asset during Dan's playing days at Western and later when he was playing for the Hamilton Tiger Cats.

Dan fit right in at Western, and in 1971 played a big role in their successful season, which culminated in a College Bowl victory over the University of Alberta. He spoke highly of Coach Frank Cosentino: "What a great guy he was."

Doug Hayes coached the offensive and defensive lines at Western. Dan remembers him as being a tough, no-nonsense coach. He enjoys telling a story about Doug, which he heard from his teammate Dave Doherty, who helped coach the Mustangs in 1972. Dave told Dan about how Doug would push Frank Cosentino to cut players who weren't making the grade:

> Doug would say, 'He's just no good, Frank. You gotta cut him.' Frank would come back with, 'I think we should give him another chance.' Doug would bounce back and say, 'NO! Cut him.'"

Dan praises his coaches at McGill and Western for teaching him the game of football. Since he only played one year of high school ball, he learned the game from the great coaching he had at two very competitive universities.

A Rookie with the Ticats

Dan had been selected in the second round of the 1971 CFL draft by the Calgary Stampeders but ended up with the Hamilton Tiger Cats in the summer of 1973.

He remembers some of the tougher parts of adjusting to playing in the CFL. In particular, he recalls a scrimmage in practice on a particularly hot summer day in Hamilton:

> We were having a big scrimmage, and I think the temperature was around 105 that day...or at least that's what it was down on the field. I was side-by-side with Gord McColum during the entire 90 minutes of that scrimmage. I remember when it was over I felt dizzy and was looking for something to grab hold of. They wouldn't give you water back then, so we were all pretty dehydrated. It seems like it took 20 minutes to walk the 40 yards to the dressing room. Once I got there, I sat down next to the big jug of Gatorade and just started pounding it down. I was so tired I couldn't lift my arms up above my shoulders for 15 minutes. I finally got my stuff off and when I did I sat down, I downed another five quarts. When my strength came back, I wandered over to the scales to weigh myself. Even with all the fluids I had just poured down my throat, I was still down 16 pounds.

After a week in training camp, Dan remembers being more tired than he had every been at McGill or Western.

Dan also has vivid memories of his first game in a Ticat uniform:

> The first game I played in Hamilton was the CFL All-Star game. That was the game where CFL All-Stars played the winner of the previous year's Grey Cup. I was on the kickoff team, and in the very first play of the game I was running down the field when all of sudden the lights went out. When I looked up from the ground, I saw this face looming over me. It was Bill Baker, the guy they called 'the undertaker.' Bill looked down at me and said, 'Welcome to the CFL, rook.' That was one of two times in my football career when I saw exploding stars.

Baker was inducted to the Canadian Football Hall of Fame in 1994 and, in 2006, was listed at #43 on the TSN Top 50 CFL Players list. His credo was "your opponents are only as tough as you let them be."

Leaving the CFL to Pursue His Career in Dentistry

Dan started at defensive tackle for two years in Hamilton, but the third year was a little different. He was commuting from the campus at Western where he was still in dental school, when he decided to hang 'em up:

Ralph Sazio called me to find out where the hell I was. I told him that I was hoping he'd offer me a hundred thousand or something. Ralph responded by saying, 'Well, good luck to you. You're suspended.' I'm still suspended today.

After that, he started his dental practice in Dunnville, Ontario, and has enjoyed a long career in dentistry ever since.

Would You Do It Again? "In a Heartbeat."

I think if I were playing again, my workout program would involve running more stairs. That's the best exercise. If there was only one exercise I could do, that would be it. You gotta have those wheels and be in top shape. Once you get out of football, if you get down and out, you bounce right back up and go at it again.

I could sit around for days exchanging stories. It was a fun game, but it taught me a lot about things, too. You find out that you weren't the only one who was a little apprehensive at times in the face of those bullets flying by your ears.

THE END COMES QUICK

Paul Kilger #74
University of Ottawa – Defensive Lineman
First Team All-Canadian 1971 and 1975

Paul Kilger earned a reputation as being one of the most disruptive defensive linemen in Canada during his five years with the Ottawa Gee-Gees. He was selected First Team All-Canadian twice and played on the 1975 Gee-Gee team that won the Vanier Cup. In 1975, he was runner-up for the top lineman of the year award in Canada.

Remembrances of Coach Rick Forrester

Paul was born and raised in Cornwall, Ontario and played football for Coach Rick Forrester at St. Lawrence High School. Coming out of high school, he attended a football camp and, as a result, was recruited to play football for Tennessee Tech in Cookville, Tennessee. During spring camp in 1971, he suffered an injury and subsequently returned to Cornwall to "rethink [his] future." During the summer of 1971, being unsure if he wanted to go to university, Paul called one of his friends, only to find out that the friend had left for the University of Ottawa football camp. He asked his friend's mother to have her son call when he had time, and the next day Paul received a phone call from Don Gilbert, the head coach for the University of Ottawa football team and said, "From that point on, I was a Gee-Gee."

Paul didn't start playing football until he was in grade 11. The first time he tried out for it was for a junior football team. He remembered being cut from the team and immediately walking to the other end of the football field where the high school football team was practicing.

He said that Coach Forrester allowed him to try out even though he had never played football before, and Paul ended up being their starting defensive end:

> I guess that's why I have such great respect for this gentleman. I had never played football in my life, and he gave me a chance. That's all we really want in life...someone to give us a chance.
>
> I've been blessed to play for a number of great coaches in my career, but I can honestly say that Coach Forrester was truly the greatest influence of my life in regards to athletics. He was one of those guys who instilled discipline, and, at the same time, values. As kids, we were looking for models. Coach Forrester was a giant in the community of Cornwall. He was greatly respected, and, as it turns out, became a good friend of mine. You could tell by his demeanor, his desire, and behaviour that winning was important...but it wasn't at all costs. He had a great influence on my life. I had a great deal of respect for the man and still do.

The 1971 Season

Paul recalls that the Gee-Gees had a fairly young team in 1971:

> I earned a starting position my first year because of my quickness. I remember that our coach, Don Gilbert, used to approach the officials before the game and tell them, 'Our defensive tackle, number 71, is extremely quick.' He told them, 'It's going to look like 71 is offsides, but he isn't; he's just very quick.'

The play-by-play announcer for the home games used to refer to Paul as the "Cornwall Cat."

He remembers playing the University of Toronto and a time when he "almost killed" Wayne Dunkley. He recalls breaking through the line just as Wayne was rolling out of the pocket to the right:

> I was in hot pursuit, and I was just wishing he would stop for a second because I had a bead on him. I didn't get as much of him as I had hoped. I remember thinking that if he had just stopped for a little bit longer I would have crunched him.

Ottawa made the playoffs in 1971. They beat McMaster in the first round of the playoffs and fell to Western in the Yates Cup by a score of 13–0.

The 1975 Vanier Cup Team

The 1975 Vanier Cup Championship Team had a phenomenal season that denies comparison, and rather than attempt to recapture it in a lesser way, here's what you need to know (courtesy of multiple online websites, including Wikipedia):

> The undefeated 1975 National Championship team (11-0) is considered to be one of the most dominant in Canadian college history. That team became the first to finish with a perfect record after winning a Vanier Cup. Even to this day, the 1975 team still holds several CIS and OUA team and individual records. Players from the 1975 team were selected to the CIS All-Canadian team 13 times during their college careers. During their CIS careers, players from the 1975 team were selected as OUAA and OQIFC All-Stars 42 times.
>
> A total of 21 players from the 1975 Vanier Cup Championship Team were selected in the Canadian Football League draft, including nine players in the first round or higher, including six CFL Territorial Protections (from 1973 through 1982, each CFL team was allowed to pick and protect two players from their region before the first round began). During their careers as professionals, players from the 1975 Vanier Cup Championship Team appeared in 23 Grey Cup games and went on to collect a total of 12 Grey Cup Rings.

The Gee-Gees defeated the University of Calgary in the Vanier Cup by a score of 14–9. Paul recalls the adverse conditions that had to be overcome to win that game:

> It was a low scoring game, partially because the game was played in freezing rain. We lost our starting quarterback in the first quarter, and he was replaced by a rookie quarterback who had played very little all year. Our starting offensive guard was also lost to injury, and Neil Lumsden sustained an injury as well. The 1975 team was inducted into the Gee-Gees Hall of Fame and attempts are being made to have the team inducted into the Canadian Football Hall of Fame.

Regrets

Paul said that his only regret was that he never got to play his natural position, which he felt was as a linebacker:

> I never weighed more than 215 pounds, which was not big for a defensive lineman, and with my quickness and upper body strength, I felt that I was better suited to be a linebacker. I ended up on the defensive

line because we were short of defensive linemen my rookie year in Ottawa. By the time I was in my fifth year, we had so many great linebackers, and I had done so well on the line, that there was nowhere else I was going to play.

Paul was drafted by the BC Lions, but, due to his size, he never made it out of training camp. He recalls getting an opportunity to show his stuff one day in camp, though:

> One of the starting defensive linemen got hurt in practice, and the coach called for another defensive lineman to step in. The line coach called for the 'Kilger kid,' and I jumped in. After practice that day, the coach came up to me and said, 'If you weighed 230 or 235 pounds, you could play d-line in this league.' I replied with a disappointed, 'Thanks.'"

Career

After the tryout with the Lions, Paul returned to Ottawa for teacher's college and his fifth year with the Gee-Gees, the 1975 season:

> I graduated and taught elementary school for the next 26 years of my life.

Paul helped coach the linemen for the Gee-Gees from 1976 through 1978 under Head Coach Cam Innes, who was also on the 1971 All Canada Football Team. After that, he coached football again when his youngest son started to play pee wee ball. He coached pee-wee football for a year, bantam for two, and midget for one.

What the Game of Football Is Really All About

After trying to remember some of the games and some of the plays from the 1970s, Paul stopped in mid-sentence and said:

> Developing friendships...that's what it's all about. Al Moffat called me a while back and told me that the second Thursday of every month we were all going to have breakfast together. We got together to do some reminiscing and enjoy our time together. I can't remember my days on the football field because they are so irrelevant. It was a great experience and the accomplishments we achieved are great, but most of us just can't remember much about our playing days, except for the fact that we're friends and that these are moments we cherish. Everything else is hard to recall. Football is the vehicle to develop friendships.

John Danaher #64

University of New Brunswick – Defensive Tackle
First Team All-Canadian – 1971

The Biggest Influence

As you've probably already discovered, as athletes all of our influences were different (although many of us credit our coaches for much of what we learned). When I asked **John** about his biggest football influence, he was quick to attribute it to his father:

> My father had played football himself and just about made the Montreal Alouettes in the late 1940s. He was the last one cut from the team, and never played football after that. But we always had a football in our back yard, and we were always tossing it around.

John's father was a fanatic about football. He loved the sport and coached football and did whatever he could to stay close to the game:

> I loved my father's direction in the sport, so football was kind of engrained in me from an early age.

Early Days in Montreal

John grew up in Montreal and started playing in the minor football association at the age of nine:

> I had some tremendous experiences playing minor football, like winning the championship and things like that—the kind of things you remember over the years.

John continued to play minor football up until he entered high school in grade eight, at which time he entered Loyola High School in Montreal and began playing football for the Warriors:

> I met some unbelievable people, but the number one person I met, as a coach, was a guy by the name of Dan Underwood.

John spoke of Coach Underwood in glowing terms as Dan played professional football in the Continental League for the Montreal Beavers in the mid-1960s while coaching high school football. After John graduated from high school, Coach Underwood moved on to become the head football coach at the University of New Brunswick in Fredericton.

University Delayed

John didn't go straight into university. He decided to play junior football in the Canadian junior football league for a couple of years before entering:

> It was quite a league at the time. In eastern Ontario and Quebec, junior football was rough and tumble football. We played against university teams in exhibition games, and we stood toe-to-toe with them. We beat them sometimes, but they also beat us, too.

John's coach in junior football was Brian Hayes, another man he holds in high regard.

Moving on to UNB and Coach Underwood

Dan Underwood must have seen the potential in John because he recruited him to play for the University of New Brunswick. As John recalls:

> Dan was an unbelievable coach and ultimately moved on to coach for Arizona State. He had spent a few years building the program at UNB by the time I arrived.

John felt that he was an "add on" player as UNB had many fine players, including Tony Proudfoot, who went on to play for many years in the CFL. Dickie Flynn was also on the team. Dickie stuck it out for a number of years with the Edmonton Eskimos before leaving to join the RCMP.

In 1970, UNB had a strong team. They won the East, but lost to Ottawa by a score of 24–13 in the Atlantic Bowl, which was played in Huskies Stadium in Halifax. 1971 was John's last year to play for the Varsity Reds. Dan Underwood had moved on to Arizona, and Jim Born was now the head coach.

John felt he was lucky to have been coached by such great men:

> You meet some amazing coaches when you play sports. Jim Born was terrific; Dan Underwood was sensational, and Brian Hayes was fantastic. Most importantly, through football, you meet people that you play with and play against. You get to know them, and you network with them while you are playing as well as later in life.

"You Realize Football Brings out the Best in a Lot of People."

John says that he still keeps in touch with the guys he played with 40 years ago, adding, "It's just sort of neat to do that."

Two years ago the University of New Brunswick recognized all of their All-Canadians over the years, in every sport. It was a huge event. They presented each athlete with a plaque commemorating their achievement. John was unable to attend and was saddened to learn that four of the seven football players who were recognized had passed on. When he thinks of all those athletes over the years, he reflects on how the game has changed:

> We were good athletes who happened to play football; today, the players are all specialists at their positions. The offensive linemen weigh 300 pounds now and don't need to run 40 yards in under five seconds because they are only concerned with the first eight yards.

Like many of the 1971 All-Canadians, John played more than one sport in high school. He played basketball but focused exclusively on football in college.

Beyond UNB

John coached basketball during his years as a high school teacher. He recalls how all the schools in his area had dropped their football programs due to issues with insurance. Then, as a principal at Cornwall Collegiate, John brought back the football program in 2002. He is proud to say that there are now six high schools in the area playing football:

> We had to rebuild the whole programme again and work on raising the calibre of the league. It takes a while, and it took us five or six years to build a respectable programme. But nothing brings a school together like football. Basketball is a great sport, and I love it, but it doesn't galvanize a school like football does. In football, you have the cheerleaders and several other school organizations that bring all the kids together.

John didn't coach football during the rebuilding years because he was the school principal, and there were several teachers and men from the community who were anxious to get involved, but he did value his time as a coach:

> It's amazing what coaching the kids does for you as a person. You get to know them on a whole different level. You feel comfortable with them and understand how they look at things. And, of course, you have something to offer them.
>
> It's remarkable…and quite an experience. I wouldn't trade any of my coaching days for anything. I loved the whole concept of coaching kids; it's fantastic.

Time Stands Still…Sort of

Even years later, players who John has coached will occasionally run into him (figuratively speaking). John reflects on how these chance encounter reflect relationships that are still built on respect:

> Once in a while, I'll bump into someone I coached in basketball in 1990. He may be balding 50 pounds heavier, but he'll still talk to me as if playing sports was the most fantastic time in his life, and he'll tell me how much respect he has for me. We don't get a lot of thank yous in our business and in our life, but those are the kind you get when you coach a kid. You learn to appreciate them when you get them. Twenty years later, you learn that you had a big impact on someone that you never knew you had.

The Football Take-Aways

The first thing I've always thought about football are the two things I've always considered myself good at: goal setting and accomplishing tasks, or at least trying to accomplish them. That all comes from teamwork and playing football. The networking that is done, and the need to rely on people to get things accomplished, is integral to football. You learn that success involves hard work and that you must rely on your judgement.

I believe football gave me the ability to work with others on any teamwork assignment. You have to work together and draw upon each other to achieve a goal. When I look back at football, I recall that there was a lot of planning and thinking that went on in order to reach our goals.

I attribute what I learned to my upbringing. I learned early on to listen to people, to listen to your coaches, and to work with others to get stuff done. I learned a lot by listening, and I mean constructively listening, to coaches.

No team can be successful because of one person; it can't happen.

I wasn't the guy that scored the touchdown that won the game, but I may have been involved in a tackle on the one-yard line that saved a game. I never thought of being the one guy, but more that I was part of the team that made the stop.

Careers

John didn't have a singular career; he had a number of them.

I had a chance to do different things in my career, and I am very lucky in terms of how things worked out.

When he graduated from UNB, he had a tryout with the Montreal Alouettes, and then he went straight into teaching. He taught for a couple of years and went back to school to obtain a master's degree. He then started working for the penitentiary system. After a few years, he had an opportunity to go into business with Xerox and worked there for 10 years in the late 70s.

When a chance came along to move back into education, he made the move and ultimately became a school vice principal and then a principal at a secondary school. He retired two years ago.

And Most Importantly...

John could not complete the story of his life without mentioning his family:

I was lucky to marry my wife Susan, who has been the love of my life for 40 years. We have eight grandchildren and a ninth on the way. Our three kids live within an easy drive of our house. It has been phenomenal.

Max Abraham #9

University of Saskatchewan – Defensive End
First Team All-Canadian 1969, 1970, and 1971

Max was born and raised in Cabri, Saskatchewan, a small town in the southwest corner of Saskatchewan about 36 miles northwest of Swift Current, which Max says is "Prairie dog country." The town's school only had about 300 students, and there were only 10 boys in his class, so the school did not have a football team.

Inspiration to Play Sports

Max attributes much of his motivation to play sports, and particularly to play football, to his best friend, Barrie Reid. Barrie and Max participated in track and field growing up in Cabri. Max was a pole vaulter and a thrower, and Barrie was a runner and high jumper. Despite coming from a small town and having to coach themselves in the sport, both Barrie and Max were successful and did well in provincial competition.

Since Cabri had no formal football programs, Max, Barrie and friends grew up playing self-organized football without equipment. This was okay when they were younger, but as they got older, some of the boys started experiencing broken collar bones, so they had to scale back their football and concentrate on track and field:

> We were fairly successful competing against the city boys, enough that it helped to build our confidence to play football with them. On one

of our trips, we met some of the guys who played for the Hilltops, the junior football team in Saskatoon. Competing in track and field at the provincial level gave us the motivation to try out for the Hilltops. I wrote a letter to the coach in the summer of 1966, and I remember him writing back and telling me that if I was interested I better hurry up because practice had already started.

Max journeyed up to Saskatoon to join the Hilltops, and Barrie joined him the next year.

Playing for the Hilltops

Max was big enough and strong enough to play for the Hilltops despite not having played organized football. This didn't bother him because he felt he was taught the proper techniques from the very beginning.

The Hilltops had a very competitive football program, and in 1968 they won the Canadian junior championship defeating the Ottawa Sooners by a score of 27–19. The coach of the Hilltops was Al Ledingham:

> Al was a very fine fellow and coach. He and Assistant Coaches Barry Mooney and Paul Schoenals were highly supportive of us, given we did not have much knowledge of the game. Both Barrie and I were proud of our ability to play competitively when we had never played high school football. Probably neither of us would have played football past high school had it not been for each of us motivating the other in track and field, and that carried on into football.

Barrie and Max both moved on to play football for the University of Saskatchewan. Barrie played one year, and Max played three.

Playing Days at the University of Saskatchewan

Both Barrie and Max had an opportunity to try out for the Saskatchewan Roughriders in the CFL after they finished playing for the Hilltops. Max decided not to try out, but Barrie did. He could catch a ball as well as anybody in the pros, but he lacked that extra step that the pros had. Coach Ledingham and his assistants had moved over from the Hilltops to coach the University of Saskatchewan Huskies, so it was easy for Max and Barrie to follow them.

Max played a different position each year he played for the Huskies, and he was selected to the All-Canadian team at all three positions: defense tackle, linebacker, and defensive end. He was a defensive player, but he did play some at fullback his first year with the Huskies. Barrie was also selected to the All-Canadian team in 1969, the only year he played university ball. He then started teaching. Max only played for three years because of a couple of injuries he sustained. He broke a small bone in his wrist while playing rugby between his first and second year. It took almost two years for his wrist to heal. Max says, "I wore a fiberglass cast on my right wrist the last two years I played."

The next injury came when he was tackling one of the Husky fullbacks during practice:

> I sustained a severe burner in my neck. I continued to play for the rest of my second year, but I had to modify my 'head first' style of tackling and adopt more of a rugby style. My third year, I was moved to defensive end, which enabled me to control opponents more with my arms, and I was less likely to reinjure myself.

By the time Max reached his fourth year, he was pretty beat up. He was also newly married, so he decided to forgo his last two years of eligibility. He did help coach the Huskies that next year before graduating.

The Huskies in the Late 60s

In the late 60s and early 70s, the Huskies were made up of a lot of lads from Saskatoon and a number of players who had come up from Regina that had played for the Rams:

> There were some older, more mature guys with junior experience, and a lot of young men from rural Saskatchewan. Those fellows that had grown up on the farm...they knew how to be tough. We didn't have a big team by any means, but defensively we were a hard hitting one. We usually won two or three games out of eight. We didn't have a real strong offense, so we would keep the games close with our defense.

A Different Era with Different Sized Players

I always laugh when I think back to those days. We had a guy weighing 180 pounds playing defensive tackle, and he was effective. We played in a time before players started to regularly lift weights. Back then, there weren't many really big players.

Max weighted about 205 pounds when he played and said he had good strength and was reasonably quick for the first five yards off the ball:

I always felt that if the guy across the line from me was a big guy I didn't have to worry as much. The guys I worried about the most were the guys my size who were equally strong and quick.

Would You Do It Again?

Max says, "I always loved football from the time I was a little guy watching the CFL on TV. It was hard work, but I loved the physicality of the game, the rewards, and the camaraderie." He also has some vivid memories of the last game he played:

I remember thinking, 'Here we are, over the ball. The opposing quarterback is calling signals. Everybody's quiet. Nobody's moving.' All is so calm and yet you know that in a the next few seconds all hell is going to break loose. That anticipation, that feeling...I knew that I was never going to experience that again. There aren't many things in life that give you that feeling on a regular basis. That excitement of the game I have certainly always missed. So...would I do it again? Yup.

The Impact of Football

Max would agree with many other players on our team that playing football definitely had an impact on his career:

When you start teaching and you really don't know a lot, you rely on what you do best, and what I did best was motivate people. I was full of energy and 'let's get at it guys.' I took that to my teaching. It worked especially well with the middle year kids who needed that. Even though I didn't know much about the art and science of instruction, I was able to bring confidence and energy there, and the kids told me about that. The importance of team work, supporting and encouraging all, and developing self-reliance are powerful learnings I also learned from football.

Where Is He Now?

Max received his degree in Education and took a job as a middle school teacher after graduation. He didn't get involved in football after he left the University of Saskatchewan because his "other love" was environmental education and outdoor education. He spent the extra hours coaching at school and developing the capacity in his school and division in environmental education.

Just three years after beginning his teaching career, he became a vice principal. He took a break for one year to serve as an environmental education consultant for the province, a field which he was passionate about. After going back to school for his master's degree, Max became a principal in a K–8 school and continued in that role for the last 15 years of his career.

After 30 years in public education, Max retired and spent the next three years managing the Partners of Saskatchewan River Basin Watershed organization. After that, he and his wife, Dalice, moved her grandparents old homestead house from Cabri to Pike Lake, 30 kilometers south of Saskatoon. They lovingly restored it and now live there. Max and Dalice have three children and seven grandchildren. Their two sons, David and Brady, both played football for the Hilltops.

THE END COMES QUICK

George Hill #26

University of Western Ontario – Linebacker
First Team All-Canadian 1971

George grew up in the Toronto area. He spent his early years living in Hyde Park, but his family moved to North York before he entered high school. He started playing football at Emery Collegiate in grade 9. It was only the second year that the school had been in existence, and it was the first year the school had a football team. George says he was lucky to have walked into that situation because it resulted in him playing five years of senior football.

Great Experience at Emery Collegiate

His first year at Emery, George weighed 155 pounds and played guard and defensive end. He actually scored the first touchdown in Emery's history when he recovered a fumble in the end zone. In his second year, he was moved to running back and outside linebacker. The team did not win a game in the first two years, but by George's fifth year they had improved significantly, and he was selected to the Toronto All-Star team. He recalls scoring five touchdowns in one game, which at the time was a record in the Toronto area.

John Metras and the Western Mustangs

One of his coaches at Emery was a graduate of the University of Western Ontario. He connected George with John Metras, the legendary coach at Western, known as "The Bull." Coach Metras invited George to a training camp, but he didn't really know what to expect as no one in his family had ever gone to university. He drove his mother to London Ontario to visit the campus of the University of Western Ontario:

> When we drove onto the campus and up to the football stadium, I felt like we were driving onto a movie set. It was quite an incredible experience for both of us.
>
> I guess I was lucky again as I played five years at Western. The first two years I was a running back, but the first year I played mostly on the specialty teams. I didn't get a lot of offensive play until we were playing McGill at our Homecoming game. I think we were up 35–0, and Coach Metras apparently thought I should have a chance to run with the ball. The first time I carried the ball I ran for a 65-yard touchdown, and John gave me shit when I came off the field because I missed the hole. The second time I touched the ball I went for 35 yards on a draw and another touchdown, but it was called back on a holding penalty.
>
> I got to play more in my second year as the starting running back. But at the beginning of my third year the coaches asked me to move to defense. They wanted me to play middle linebacker in a new for UWO 4–3 defense. So, I made the move and played my remaining three years on defense. We had great defense in those three years. I was fortunate to be in the right place at the right time surrounded by outstanding teammates.

Coach Metras let go of the reins as the head football coach after George's third year, and Frank Cosentino became the new head coach. Frank had been released from his contract with the Toronto Argonauts to accept the teaching and coaching job at Western. In that first year, he appointed George team captain, which resulted in a very special relationship between the two men.

Success After Turning Down the CFL

Western had a great team in 1970, and many thought it was better than the 1971 team. George said, "We felt that if we had made the playoffs we would have gone quite far, but we missed the playoffs by a point."

I was drafted by Ottawa and went to their camp. I stayed around until the intersquad game, at which time I asked Frank Clare if he thought I would start. He told me he didn't think so, but he wanted me to stay around on the taxi team. I wasn't prepared to do that. I really didn't think that professional football and me were meant to be. I wasn't committed enough to do some of the things that they wanted done. I decided to go back to Western and try to get into Althouse Teacher's College. I was fortunate to get accepted, and that's how I made it onto the 1971 team.

George felt he was very lucky indeed to get accepted into Althouse, the teacher's college connected to the University of Western Ontario, as they usually required students to apply early, and he showed up very late. Fortunately, they found a place for him. He had been a Physical Education major with a minor in history. The school informed George that the history section was filled up and asked him if he had any other specialties. He told them that he had driven a Pepsi truck in the summers and deliver Pepsi. Someone figured out that driving a Pepsi truck had something to do with business, so they admitted George into the business section. He said he was lucky again because he was able to secure his first teaching job at Georgetown DHS because he had the business and the physical education combination:

> Football has been intertwined in my whole life since I was 13 years old. I was not involved much with football after my playing years, but football led me to my career, which lasted 33 years. Most importantly, it also helped me find my best friend and wife of 45 years, Diane.

Developing Core Skills

George's high school football coach, whom he played under for five years, had played for the Toronto Argonauts and provided him with a sound football foundation. He feels he could not have had two better coaches to play for in university than John Metras and Frank Cosentino.

Remembering the 1971 Season

George has very vivid memories of the 1971 season because it was such a successful season, culminating in Western winning the College Bowl:

It was like two seasons. We fiddled around during the regular season. McMaster beat us on a last second field goal, and we lost the last game against Windsor. We knew that Windsor would have to beat us by something like 36 points for us not to make the playoffs. We were very unfocused in that Windsor game. Our starting cornerback broke his arm, and our starting defensive end broke his leg. On top of that, our starting outside linebacker was ejected from the game for arguing with the referee. But in the final four games we were a different team. We only had two touchdowns scored on us in those four games, and the offense overpowered the opposing defenses.

George recalls that the McMaster game was a pivotal game in the season. Prior to that game, the starting offensive and defensive units scrimmaged against third team players in practice. After the loss to McMaster, the team had a closed team meeting, which resulted in George having a meeting with Frank Cosentino and requesting that the starting offense scrimmage against the starting defense in practice. Frank agreed, and the rest is history.

George could not say enough nice things about Frank Cosentino: "I could talk for hours about Frank; he's a great man!"

George accomplished something very unusual for university sports, which was that Frank let him call every defensive play in the two years that George was Captain and starting middle linebacker:

> No one ever second-guessed me. I never came off the field and had one of the coaches say, 'That was a dumb ass thing to do.' I learned from that how important it was to trust your people. Get them trained, put your trust in them, and let them do their job. Don't second-guess them.

Career

George spent three years as a teacher and coached high school football at Georgetown District High School. He figured that the principal hired him because he knew football, and their football program had been struggling. George was able to turn that around, and by the time he was finished, the team was in the playoffs.

George left teaching after three years because he realized that working to rule was not for him. He had always been interested in business and finance and had spoken to his UWO linebacker coach, Ron Potter, about a career with London Life at one point. When he decided to leave teaching, George called Frank Cosentino and asked him if he knew anyone in Toronto that was in the life insurance business. Frank put him in touch with Bill Bartlett, a former teammate of Frank's from Western, and George went to work selling life insurance for Aetna.

George spent the rest of his career in the finance and insurance business and spent the last 10 years of his career running Allstate Canada:

> Football definitely helped me in my career. Teamwork and esprit de corps are essential in football and in business. To be successful in both, you have to have a good team that is working toward the same goal. You want a focused team, one in which everyone knows their job, and you must have confidence that each of them can do those jobs. Team sports teaches you a lot about interpersonal skills, like making sure you recognize people. There are all sorts of parallels.

Where Is He Now?

George and his wife Diane currently spend half the year living in New Zealand and the other half living in Muskoka watching their grandchildren grow. They believe that they could not have found two more beautiful places to live.

Gill Bramwell #31

University of Manitoba – Linebacker
First Team All-Canadian – 1971

Gill Bramwell played on two Vanier Cup championship teams, was selected to the first CIS All Canada Football Team, and is one of the winningest high school coaches in Manitoba. What he cherishes most through it all are the relationships he built with his teammates and the players he coached.

Gill grew up in Winnipeg and started his football career with the St. Vital Mustangs when he was 10 years old. He played with the Mustangs all the way up to 'juvenile,' which had players as old as 18 or 19 at the time. Gill played quarterback and linebacker with the Mustangs. Eventually the juvenile program amalgamated with junior football in Winnipeg.

Playing for the University of Manitoba

Gill had always wanted to play for the Bisons, so when he finished playing for the Mustangs he submitted his application to the University of Manitoba and eventually met with Henry Jensen, the head coach. Everything worked out as he had hoped, and Gill showed up for practice in the fall of 1968.

Given that Bobby Kraemer was the starting quarterback for the Bisons, Gill found himself focusing on the defensive side of the ball. He started the first few games in 1968 as outside linebacker but was soon moved to middle linebacker where he played for the remainder of his career with the University of Manitoba.

Gill recalls how everyone on the team had to be able to play multiple positions as there were only 28 players on the travelling squad, and one of those players was their kicker:

> Travelling to places like Vancouver from Winnipeg back then was quite expensive. We had to be able to function at a number of different positions. If someone went down in a game, we could quickly find ourselves playing both ways.

Gill said they only had 36 players on the full-time roster:

> The coaches made an agreement with the local junior teams (I believe there were four junior teams back then), that we would not keep a lot of players on the team that were not going to see the field. It was better for the players to have a chance to play for the junior teams rather than sit on the bench with the Bisons. Times have changed though. Brian Dobie, the current Bison coach, has 75 or 80 players on his roster.

The highlight of Gill's career were the back-to-back national championships in 1969 and 1970. He said, "Being national champions was kind of exciting, and, of course, being on a winning football team in those days was pretty substantial."

In 1971, their quarterback, Bobby Kraemer, had moved on to play for the Winnipeg Blue Bombers: "We had a lot of depth from the previous years. I had a good year, and the team had a good year, but losing Kraemer hurt us."

The highlight and lowlight of the season both came against UBC:

> We were playing UBC in Winnipeg and were beating them 44–0 when our big running back, Bob Toogood, blew out his knee. A week later, we played UBC in Vancouver, and they beat us 11–8. That loss kept us from making the playoffs in 1971. I would have given up my selection to the All-Canadian team if our team would have been able to represent our conference that year.

How the Game Develops Young Men

> There was a lot of bonding with the guys whom I am still friends with today. We still meet every once in a while at Boston Pizza here in Winnipeg. Even Bobby Toogood, who played eight years for the Bombers, shows up as some of his best friends are his teammates from the Bisons. It was a very special time.

I look at the teams I played with in 1969, 1970, and 1971. A lot of those guys have gone on to success. Many of them have done very well for themselves: doctors, lawyers, dentists, school teachers. Many went into business and have done quite well.

That dedication—to task, teamwork, to pushing yourself to do your best—pays off in everyday life.

Gill believes that many of those things have to be in place for people to achieve in the sport's higher levels. He believes that as you go higher in football you see these common traits: "That's why those guys are still there."

After the Bisons

After finishing his playing career with the Bisons, Gill coached high school football for a year and then joined the Bison coaching staff. He coached the Bisons for 14 years, 10 with Head Coach Dennis Hrycaiko, a former teammate and All-Canadian with the Bisons. Gill eventually became the team's defensive coordinator.

When he left the Bisons, he was teaching at a K–9 school when he received a call from the principal at Oak Park High School in Winnipeg:

> The principal wanted me to come teach at Oak Park, and one of the primary reasons was to start a football programme. I got that going, and three years later we won the provincial championship.

Gill recruited one of the players he'd coached at the University of Manitoba to help him coach at Oak Park. That coach took over after Gill left and has since developed a junior varsity team.

Growth of Football in Winnipeg

There were only six high schools in Winnipeg in the mid-60s, and the high school in the area where Gill grew up did not have a football team:

> Of course, there are 27 teams in the city today. It's growing like crazy. Some schools still don't have teams because it requires somebody who will take the bull by the horns to get a programme going. Any high school principal who has his head on his shoulders should easily see the benefits of football for the school and the players.

Gill has been involved with high school football in Winnipeg for many years and has been key to the growth of football in Winnipeg.

They Still Call Him Coach

Gill spoke at length about the relationships that are built through playing and coaching football: "It's a life long relationship is what it is."

He spoke about how coaching in high school enables those relationships to develop to a much deeper level. Coaches are more influential when they are also teaching in high school:

> Teaching in the same school, and even having some of the boys in my classroom, allowed constant contact and enabled us to have team meetings and film sessions during the day. This level of interaction is not available in community football.

> I had some kids who were a little rough around the edges, and the only thing keeping them in school was their contact with me and being on the football team. Several of them were borderline, not knowing which way to turn.

One of Gill's borderline players went on to play university football for five years and is now working with disadvantaged youth in the city. He turned around 180 degrees.

Gill believes football is the greatest game for boys who are 15, 16, and 17 years old:

> It's the best thing for them because of the qualities that it teaches: responsibility, dedication to a task, and teamwork. It's a pretty endearing kind of sport for boys that age.

Leaving a Legacy

In the five years prior to Gill's retirement as the head football coach at Oak Park High School, the Raiders lost only three of the 55 games they played, and two of those losses came in provincial championship games. Gill lead the Raiders to three undefeated seasons and three consecutive provincial titles in his last three years as head coach.

When Gill retired from coaching, Cathy Penner, the wife of the Raider's offensive line coach, Lindsay Penner, organized a roast for him. They donated a portion of the ticket sales to the Canadian Cancer Society in memory of Gill's wife Gaye.

Jason Penner, Cathy and Lindsay's son, spoke about Gill:

> He always put his players before himself. He'd do so much for you. He always pushed me to go one step further, either academically or athletically.

Gill speaks proudly of the accomplishments of the young men he coached:

> One of the boys, Jamie Kozak, went on to work for the city as an architect. He organized a fundraiser with a number of other former Oak Park Raider football players. They raised $240,000 to put in a new field at Oak Park High School. Now, they're raising money to put in lights, so the team can play night games.
>
> Coaching football was one of the most influential parts of my entire life and it is still. My contact with players that I coached or guys that I played with continues to this day. It's that constant contact with people who have meant so much to you that I appreciate.

The End Comes Quick

Bob Eccles #34

Carleton University – Linebacker
First Team All-Canadian 1969, 1970, and 1971

Bob was born in an area of Ottawa called Mechanicsville and says, "It was literally on the other side of the tracks." Mechanicsville was mostly an Irish and French Catholic community.

> I was an English Protestant, so I chose to hang with the Irish guys because I didn't speak French. I ultimately did learn French as a means of self preservation.

Early Days and Early Setbacks

Bob's first exposure to football was in Little League with a team called the Laroche Park Tigers. They were in a league referred to as the Little Big Four because there were only four teams. He played for them for two years and then entered Champlain High School, where he played for four years.

Bob's journey from high school to Carleton University was a circuitous one. After high school, he was invited to attend a camp sponsored by the Ottawa Rough Riders, which was designed to help high school football players secure scholarships to play for U.S. universities:

> I did well and was supposed to be going to Ball State in Indiana. I waited most of the summer to hear from them and finally called Frank Clair, the GM of the Rough Riders, to find out what was going on. Frank said, 'Didn't anybody tell you? Ball State had a recruiting violation, so they had their quota of scholarships cut.' So, I was left dangling in the wind. I had turned down an offer to play for Queens.

They had an arrangement with alumni to pay for tuition and to get players jobs. Having turned that down, thinking I was going to the States, all of a sudden I had nothing.

Fortunately for Bob he had submitted an application to Carleton University the December before he graduated from high school. He was able to enroll at Carleton in the fall of 1967. He remembers walking across campus on his first day of school and walking past the football field. A few minutes later, he decided that maybe he should give football a try at Carleton.

"Eccles? What Are You Doing Here?"

When Bob met with the coach at Carleton, the coach's first reaction was, "Eccles? What are you doing here? You're supposed to be in the States." When Bob explained the situation, the coach was more than happy to put him on the team.

In 1967, St. Patrick's College had just amalgamated with Carleton, so there were two teams of players trying to make it at Carleton. Bob ended up being a backup running back to a veteran who was in his fourth year. He road the bench the first year, but better things were ahead.

In the summer of 1968, Bob was working for the City of Ottawa keeping track of gravel trucks as they brought their loads into a construction site when he received a call from Keith Harris, Carleton's football coach. Keith wanted Bob to meet him and one of the other coaches for lunch. Bob's immediate thoughts were that he had done something wrong. They met at a fast food restaurant and after a long wait, Coach Harris finally got to the point of the meeting, saying, "Bob, you are probably wondering why we called you here. We want you to play middle linebacker this year." Bob said he had to re-sculpt his body. He put on 20 pounds, going from 200 to 220, and spent the summer lifting weights:

> I never played running back again after that. I really enjoyed being a linebacker. I rather enjoyed giving punishment rather than taking it.

Remembering His Coaches

Bob describes his Champlain High School Coaches as "a great bunch of guys." George Simonet, a former football player at Queens, was his head coach. Pat McAlpine was his defensive coach:

> Real solid guys and good role models. When I was selected to the Carleton Hall of Fame, I invited my high school coaches to the ceremony, including George. He was getting frail and wasn't able to attend, but I did get to talk to him on the phone. I even had my peewee coaches there. It was great to have all of them in attendance.

At Carleton, his coach was Keith Harris:

> We were always the underdogs when we played, being a small team. Keith Harris had played at Queens under Frank Tindall and had also coached with him. He was very strategic and had all kinds of tips on angles. For instance, if a big guy is coming straight at you, you are always going to get beat, but if you can cut him low or get an angle on him and move him around, you can gain an advantage.

> The field at Carleton was named after Coach Harris. He had been big in the OUA and at one time was also its president.

What Bob Valued Most

The more I asked this question, the more often I received the same response, one shared by many of the men on the 1971 All-Canadian Team. Here's Bob's:

> When I think of the whole experience, what I valued most was just the camaraderie of the guys. It was a good group of guys who hung together and became lifelong friends. I think that's what I take away most—the personal aspect of it. Friendships. The fame and glory of the game is fleeting but hopefully you are going to be around a hell of a lot longer and will have those guys to back you up. Remember the relationships while you have them…and savor the moments.

> We had a reunion last year after more than 40 years. We met at the old tavern…and the bullshit was rolling.

Life After the 1971 Season

When the 1971 season was over, Bob's rights were still owned by the Ottawa Rough Riders, so he received a call from their GM, Frank Clair. Frank wanted Bob to come back and try out again. He offered Bob the same contract that he had offered him in 1970. Bob said that was fine, but he wanted a bonus. He reminded Frank that he had received a $500 bonus in 1970 and since he was better now, he wanted another bonus:

> Frank told me, 'No. We don't give bonuses to retreads. So I said, 'Okay, thanks. Goodbye.'
>
> After that, my rights were part of a couple of trades. I received a call from Dick Shoto in Toronto. He wanted me to come down there, and I told him I was out of football. Then, I received a call from Calgary wanting me to go out there. I told them no.
>
> Finally, one Saturday morning, I was working at a garage in Ottawa, and I was pumping gas when a guy phones me and says, 'This is Bobbie Ackles.' And I said, 'No. This is Bob Eccles. Who are you?' 'Bobbie Ackles.' 'No, no. I'm Bob Eccles.' It was like a 'Who's on First' routine. As it turned out, it was Bobbie Ackles, the GM for the BC Lions. They had obtained my rights and wanted me to come to BC.

At that point, Bob was finished with football. He had seen how the CFL worked from the inside and decided it wasn't for him. He went back to Carleton to work on another degree and decided to play hockey. He wasn't eligible to play football and had played hockey in his junior days before going to Carleton:

> So, that was it for playing football. I coached at the peewee and midget level for the Myers Riders. The second year, Paul Kilger showed up, and we coached the team together. We won the Ontario championship the last year I coached.

Bob got involved with the "Old Crows Society" at Carleton for football alumni. Through the Old Crows, he started announcing the home games for the Ravens, which he continued to do for 10 years:

> That was when Ace Powell was there. He wanted to get as many former players involved as he could. We were announcing the games and cooking hot dogs for the society at half-time.

Lessons and Memories

The biggest lesson I took away from the game was to remember that when you get down there is always the chance to come back. If you keep trying and are persistent and have the will to win, you can turn things around. And, if you don't make it, keep trying because there's always another chapter if the current one doesn't turn out, and you learn from your mistakes. Competition doesn't mean you're going to win all the time, but it means you can compete all the time.

Bob shared a comical memory from a game against their archrivals, the Ottawa Gee-Gees, in their annual "Panda Game." His coach, Pete Thompson, had played in the CFL for Toronto and Ottawa. Pete had played with a guy named Tom Brown, who was a middle guard on defense. One of Tom's favorite plays was to beat the snap count and run into the opposing team's center on a punt play. In one of Carleton's games against the Gee-Gees, things were getting crazy on the field, and Pete Thompson looked at Bob and said, "Tom Brown."

Bob took his instructions, jumped offside, and ran into the center. He said the center rolled backwards into the backfield, and Carleton received a five-yard penalty. On the next play, the center snapped the ball over the punter's head, and Bob recovered the ball for Carleton. Pete and Bob relive this story every time they get together.

Would He Do It Again?

If I had it all to do over again, I would slow it down and enjoy the experience more. Other than that, I wouldn't change much. I'd just let it happen. There were a lot of negatives, but when you add the total up, it's a big positive: a life experience, steel forged under fire.

Career and Family

Bob spent his career working in the health, safety, and personnel arena and still does some consulting in this area. As he says, "I am semi-retired, but I still keep my foot in the door."

Bob's wife, Sharon, passed away a couple of years ago. He and Sharon were married for 37 years. He has two amazing children who have been very successful. His daughter, Gina, was an Olympic athlete on the weightlifting team and currently works in Calgary as a physiotherapist for professional and Olympic athletes. Bob's son, Robbie, played football and hockey growing up. Robbie also competed in Bike Polo and at one time was rated third in the world. Robbie currently has his own business doing renovations.

Bob has recently connected with some of his former teammates, and they are getting together to relive old times:

> Other than that, I am enjoying life as much as I can right now...and trying to add value to society through Buddhism.

Glenn Ponomarenko #73

University of Saskatchewan – Linebacker
First Team All-Canadian – 1971

Glenn was born in Biggar, Saskatchewan, and spent his early years there. Biggar is located about 90 kilometers west of Saskatoon and is known for its town motto: "New York is Big, but this is Biggar."

High School and Junior Football

Glenn and his family moved to Saskatoon by the time he was ready for high school, and he played high school ball in Saskatoon and then moved on to play for the Saskatoon Hilltops, which was one of Canada's premier junior football programs. Glenn played linebacker for the Hilltops who won the "Little Grey Cup" in 1968 and 1969. He recalls defeating Kelowna for the championship in 1968 and the Ottawa Sooners in 1969.

Glenn received a partial scholarship offer to play for Simon Fraser University but found it more convenient to stay in Saskatoon and play for the University of Saskatchewan. He said many of the players from the Hilltops went on to play for there. He played for the U of S for three years, from 1970 through the 1972 season.

The Best Memories and One Regret

The 1971 season was not a particularly good year for us. We had a 2–6 season, which was frustrating for the players, the coaches, and the spectators. We had great coaches and great players. There were a lot of rookies on the team that year and many close games, but we just couldn't rack up the wins.

One game in particular stands out for Glenn, a game against the University of Alberta:

> We lost a heartbreaker by one point on a last second field goal. I remember because I was on the line and watched the ball sail over my head and through the uprights...and that was it.

The University of Alberta went on to make the playoffs that year and ultimately played Western in the College Bowl in Toronto.

The most vivid memories of his time playing with the University of Saskatchewan are of his teammates:

> I recall that we had a great group of guys that loved to play football and played for the love of the game. We even loved practicing. We had a head coach named Al Ledingham who was a slave driver, but he was a very knowledgeable football coach. He drove us hard. When I look back on it now, I realize what he was trying to do. He made us better players and better individuals.

Glenn spoke of the team's camaraderie in glowing terms. He reflected on their tradition of going to a local pub after every game, whether they won or lost:

> Some of those times were really great! We would rehash the game, saying things like, 'Great play. I saw you smack that guy. Great job.' Unfortunately, in the moment, we didn't realize we needed to cherish those times more. I wish I had more memories, some game films, some clippings—more mementos from that era, so I could look back at them and reminisce. That was a very closely knit group. We would've done anything for each other.

> One of the regrettable things is that we never made it to the playoffs, let alone the Vanier Cup.

The Good Times

When it comes to memories of specific plays or games, Glenn, like many others, has a difficult time remembering individual plays or game situations. He made an interesting observation though:

> When you think of the whole experience of playing football, collectively, you think of the good times. There were a lot of those. You can't

put your finger on any one particular incident, but you remember when you were singing away, having a beer. You'd go into the pub at seven o'clock, and suddenly it was midnight. Where the hell did the five hours go? The other thing is that we were treated very well by the population, the sports writers, and the radio stations. We had a lot of good press, win or lose, and the feeling we got was that we were doing our job.

The Trouble with Contacts

One of his funniest memories of his playing days had to do with his contact lenses:

> I used to play in contact lenses. Back then, they were hard lenses, and they were really expensive compared to what you pay for them today. There were a few times that I hit someone, and one of my lenses popped out. We would have to stop the game, and everybody would get down on their hands and knees to look for my lens in the grass. Once, when one of them popped out, I didn't have my saline solution, so I put it in my mouth to clean it with saliva. As soon as I did, someone cracked a joke; I hiccupped and swallowed the lens. Fortunately, I had a backup pair, but it was like having a $100 meal without the calories. I filed an insurance claim for the loss of the lens as I wasn't about to sift through poop for the next several days looking for the damn thing.

Friendly Rivalries

The friendly rivalries that existed on the team between offense and defense and between the offensive line and defensive line were a great source for fond memories. Glenn remembered how the coaches would protect the quarterback even putting a red jersey on him in practice to keep him from getting hurt. Every once in a while, the quarterback would get knocked down, though, and the coaches would go nuts... but the defense would get in the huddle and laugh about what just happened.

> I also loved playing with Max Abraham. We would gang up on the center from time to time. Both of us would just smack this guy a couple of plays in a row, and, rest assured, his future snaps would be a little on the wobbly side.

Reckless Abandon

Glenn told his racquetball buddies that he couldn't play football with today's rules:

> When I played football, I played with reckless abandon. I wasn't there to hurt anybody, but I was there to knock them down. That was my job. If I had to stop halfway through a tackle to determine if my shoulder was in the right place or if my head was up before I smacked a guy, I couldn't play.

Glenn attributes the fact that he made it through his football career without any significant injuries to the way he played, saying, "If I had to stop and think about what I was doing, I would have gotten hurt."

Coaches

> Al Ledingham was my coach and mentor. He coached us at the Hilltops and then came over with us to the University of Saskatchewan. We weren't buddy buddies, but we sure had a lot of respect for him. If he asked us to run through a brick wall, we would say, 'Do you want us to hit it high or low?' The man just had a tremendous work ethic. He put us through our paces when it came to the physical aspect of the game and taught us the techniques and finer points as well. Our working relationship was one of great respect and admiration. He's still alive and kicking, and to this day I still talk to him and email him. I sometimes think that players don't thank their coaches enough, so I tell him from time to time that he was the best coach ever!

Being Selected for the All-Canadian Team

Glenn has a very vivid memory of when he found out that he had been selected to the All Canada Football Team:

> I was in a bar. The local sportswriter came in and said, 'Congratulations, Glenn! You made the all-star team. I didn't think you were going to make it, but you did, so congratulations.' I thought he was referring to the Canada West All-Star Team, so I didn't think much of it at the time. A few days later, I found a copy of the newspaper article and saw that I had been selected to the All Canada team.

Football's Long-Term Impact

There are many people who might have ended up in jail if it weren't for sports. Life likes to knock you down, but football teaches you to get back up. I learned to surround myself with good people—good positive people. You've got to have the teamwork, and you've got to have the communication. Lead by example, know your job. I've always told my people, 'Once you think you know everything, it's time to get out.'

Career

After a brief stint with the Montreal Alouettes in the CFL, Glenn started his career working as a marketing representative for Gulf Oil. He worked for them for five years and then made the switch over to residential real estate.

He started out as a sales rep, then went on to become a branch manager, then an area manager, then a vice president and regional manager, and ultimately ended up with his own franchise:

> That was my career path, and everything on that path was influenced by football. It had it all—from the training, to working hard, and surrounding myself with positive people.

Glenn is retired now and still enjoying good health, claiming he has never had any serious illnesses. He says he's had a good life and uses an analogy that incorporates his football career:

> The analogy I use is like building a house. You can build a good foundation and put whatever structure you want on it. The foundation for my life was the football aspect of it, and I've built a pretty good house on top of that.

THE END COMES QUICK

Bob Mincarelli #28

St. Francis Xavier – Defensive Back
First Team All-Canadian 1971 and 1972

Bob was born in Harrison, New York, and spent his early days growing up there. His first football experience was playing youth league football when he was 10. Bob's family moved to Glastonbury Connecticut when he was 12, and he continued to play youth league ball until he was ready to enter high school.

As his freshman year approached, Bob became quite concerned about continuing his football career as Glastonbury did not have a high school football team. He played basketball and baseball, too, but he loved football. Fortunately, the townspeople in Glastonbury petitioned to have football reinstated at the high school, and Bob was able to continue his football career. 2016 marked the 50th anniversary of football in Glastonbury, and Bob is proud to say that he played on their very first team.

From the time he started playing in high school, Bob played both split end and defensive back. For most of his career, he played both ways.

Like many of those on the 1971 team, Bob had a special relationship with his coach, but it didn't start out that way:

> I thought I would have an in with the coach because I was Italian, and he was Italian, but never was I so wrong. In fact, it was probably just the opposite. The coach was a tough guy, and everyone on the team shivered when he walked on the field.

Despite the coach's toughness, Bob said:

> When I look back at the end of my career, if there were three or four guys in my life that influenced me, that coach would've had to be in

the number one or two position. He was tough and authoritarian. In that time, when we all idolized Joe Namath and his white shoes, if we wore white shoes onto the field, we might as well have stayed home. That just wasn't happening. He was old school all the way. He expected a lot, but he gave a lot. He was very dedicated to the team and his players. I had an outstanding relationship with him over time.

He died this past year. His name was Ray Nicoletta. In his latter years, he would go to the local football game every Friday night. He always sat in a special seat because he was the guy that started the programme here. I always went down and sat with him on those Friday nights and watched the games from the sideline. He was one of those special guys. I never did call him by his first name. I always called him Coach, even after all those years.

Bob's high school years were marked by a lot of firsts—the first team, the first win, the first winning season and says, "It was kind of a special time."

How He Ended Up at St. Francis Xavier

Bob played three sports and always felt that he would play one of those sports in college because he did well in all of them. He felt that baseball was his best, and he loved basketball, too. Some schools expressed an interest in him, but none of the ones he wanted to attend. In fact, Bob calls himself, "an underrecruited player." But then came the opportunity to play for St. Francis Xavier (StFX):

> I remember being called down to the athletic director's office after all the signing days had passed. He said that he wanted me to meet a college coach from a Canadian university. He encouraged me not to say 'no' before talking to him. The coach was Jim Bourne. He was a relatively new coach who had played for Michigan State, so he caught my attention. The fact that it was a Catholic university was very favorable to my parents, and everything seemed very nice from what I could see in print.

Bob went on to say that StFX was very aggressive in pursuing him after the initial meeting and that he thought of all the colleges pursuing him, this was a school that wanted him the most. He signed to play without ever seeing the campus.

Adjusting to the Canadian Game

The things I remember most about my first year include being embarrassed by not knowing all the rules and learning about the legacy of our coach, Don Loney.

Bob learned about some of the unique Canadian rules in one of his early games when he failed to field a punt, and the kicker from the opposing team recovered it. The biggest adjustment, though, was learning of Coach Don Loney's legacy. Apparently, Don liked to run up the score on his opponents. StFX had a long reputation of winning and even referred to themselves as the Notre Dame of Canadian college football. But when they had down years, their opponents got revenge by pummeling them. Bob's first year at StFX was one of those down years. He could tell by how the opponents talked to him and his teammates, and particularly what was said at the bottom of the piles, that there was a lot of animosity.

The other adjustment was the age of the players:

> My first year I was like a deer in the headlights. I was only 17 years old playing against these men. They all had moustaches, and a lot of them had beards. It took me until mid-season before I started to feel comfortable.

Some Memories, Good and Bad

> I remember some of the rivalries with other schools. The biggest game for us each year was against St. Mary's. We cracked the top 10 only once in the four years I played for StFX, and we got beat in the last game against St. Mary's, which knocked us out of the top 10.
>
> I played both ways, flanker on offense and defensive back. I kicked field goals and extra points, and I returned kicks. I did a lot of things. I remember being on the field all the time.

Bob also remembered a blow to the head he received on one pass play. He went up for the ball, caught it, and got upended in mid-air. He was flipped over and came down on his head. The blow knocked him out, but the ball rolled out of his hands and between his legs without touching the ground, so it was ruled a catch. Because he was out cold, he didn't realize he'd caught the ball:

My teammates helped me up off the ground, and I remember heading for the sideline because I felt I was injured. As I approached the sideline, I saw the coach pointing at me, and I'm sure he was saying, 'Get the 'F' back in there.' When I got back into the huddle, I told the quarterback not to throw it to me on the next play.

Football After StFX

Bob wasn't sure where he would go when he finished at StFX. Coach Loney had said that he was the best professional prospect that had come along in years, but Bob didn't realize that he was considered an import by the CFL, which explained why he didn't hear from any CFL teams. He did, however, receive a few letters from the Dallas Cowboys, but they stopped coming in the spring of his senior year.

It wasn't until his senior year that he understood the five-year rule in Canadian college football. He looked around and decided to attend teacher's college at the University of Ottawa, so he became a Gee-Gee for his fifth year. That was 1974 when the Gee-Gees went undefeated through the regular season but lost to Toronto in the playoffs. It was the first time in Bob's career that he didn't play both ways. He played flanker on offense for the first half of the season and moved to defense for the last half, based on the team's needs. He said that the 1974 Ottawa Gee-Gees team was the best team he had ever played on. The coach was Don Gilbert, and one of the defensive linemen was Paul Kilger.

The New York Giants

The exposure Bob got playing for Ottawa in his fifth year earned him a look by the New York Giants. In his words, it was "the break of a lifetime."

> I was contacted by the New York Giants to go down to what they called a mini camp. I ended up going to two mini camps, and they signed me to a free agent contract and put me down as a wide receiver. I went to the rookie camp early in the summer, made it through that camp, and was invited to their final preseason camp. I spent three or four weeks in that camp then was cut. The end comes quick. You know it's all over when they call you into the coach's office and tell you

to bring your playbook.

Career

Bob spent the better part of his career as an executive with LEGO. He worked in marketing and sales and was able to live in his hometown of Glastonbury, Connecticut throughout his career and continues to do so now in retirement. He feels strongly that his experience playing football had a great deal to do with his success in business:

> Football had a major impact on everything. When I think about the confidence I had in myself, I think about football. In the roles I had in business, they were pretty much all leadership roles, going from small to medium to very large teams over my career. It was inevitable to fall back on stuff from being involved on a team, like being a team captain and being in a semi-leadership role responsible for motivating people. To this day, when I think about managing people, I think about all the lessons coming from football—commitment, hard work, teamwork—that kind of stuff all flowed very naturally into leadership roles.
>
> Also, there's the notion of 'can do.' If you played football in college or beyond, you had to have a 'can do' attitude. There's no two ways about it. There's no choice. You didn't survive if you didn't have that.
>
> I think the parallels are unbelievable, coming out of football. It all comes down to motivating, leading, and inspiring people, and you get an awful lot of that being part of a football programme. And when you think of the other part—'can do'—overcoming obstacles and meeting challenges, again, it all flows. You can trace everything back to one pep talk or another, whatever you received from a coach.
>
> I would also add that whatever your stepping off point was from your football career, it gives you humility because you realize that while you think you're a good player, there are a lot of good players.

Where Is He Now?

Bob is retired now. Since retiring, he has coached football, taught at the local college, done a lot of fishing, and really enjoys speaking to high school students and football teams. The title of his speech is "Life's Plan."

The End Comes Quick

Rick Chevers #33

University of Waterloo – Defensive Back
First Team All-Canadian – 1971

Rick grew up in Niagara Falls, Ontario, where his father was the Chief of Police, and his grandfather was the Mayor. Despite the family ties, Rick had some rough edges growing up and tangled with the law on occasion. His brother characterized Rick's approach to life:

> He lived life to the fullest and loved a good time, on and off the field. His philosophy was: 'Go 90 miles an hour all the time and hit everything you can.' He lived hard and played hard.

Athletics and Opportunities

Like many members of the 1971 All Canada Football Team, Rick was a two-sport athlete. He excelled in both hockey and football. Many who saw him play both sports thought he could have played professional hockey in the NHL. He had an opportunity to play hockey on a college scholarship in the United States, but an accident involving an opposing player resulted in Rick shifting his focus away from the sport. He returned to Canada to play football for the University of Waterloo.

After his selection to the 1971 All Canada Football Team, Rick was chosen by the Toronto Argonauts in the first round of the CFL draft. Most felt that he would earn a spot with the Argos, but a freak accident in training camp ended any hope he had of playing professional football.

Emotions and Plenty of Friends

Rick was a sensitive guy, who wore his emotions on his sleeve, and often did the first thing that came to mind. One example of his spontaneity was a decision to walk from his cottage on the Niagara River at 2:00 a.m., crossing the U.S. border and back, all for a couple of pounds of extra-hot wings.

He had friends aplenty. Rick would give you the shirt off his back. He was always available and willing to help. All he asked for was a beer when the job was done. Friends and family loved him, saying, "When he supported you—you felt it. No doubt about it."

A Family Man <u>who</u> Loved the Water

Rick was very proud of his family. He was married for more than 30 years to Patty. They had two beautiful girls and several grandchildren. When Rick finished his working career, all he could think of was getting back to Niagara Falls to be with his children and grandchildren.

Rick loved being involved in activities on and in the water. Patty says that he would've preferred it if he could've found a way to strap a boat to his back. His first was a 16-foot fishing boat. He ultimately made it up to a 36-foot power boat, and a very large pontoon boat. He loved fishing, especially on the Niagara River. Combining fishing, boating, and a beer was heaven to Rick.

Rick had three strokes later in life, precipitated by his smoking. Patty feels that it was his smoking that led to his premature departure at age 67. He loved life to the end, leaving no challenge unmastered, no friend left wanting, nor no family member unloved.

His teammate at Waterloo, John Buda, completely agreed, saying, "That's how I remember Rick. He was a great friend, a fierce competitor, and a superb football player."

Chris Harber #8

Carleton University – Defensive Back
First Team All-Canadian 1971

The Early Days

Chris settled in Ottawa as a youngster after touring Europe and England with his parents during the post-war period. He first played football with the Belair Lions of the Little Big Four football league, the same league that Bob Eccles played in. Little did he know that he would be a teammate of Bob's at Carleton many years later.

While Chris felt he wasn't a particularly good football player, he enjoyed the physicality of the sport, the camaraderie, and the sense of belonging and being accepted into a group. He says, "In hindsight, this was an important step toward building my self identity."

Achieving Success in High School

In high school, he continued to play football in Ottawa for the Laurentian Lions under a coach named Joe Upton. Coach Upton had played for the Ottawa Rough Riders and coached at Laurentian during the late 50s and early 60s:

> He was a terrific coach, very demanding, but, at the same time, very fair. To this day, he is revered by his players. I totally respected and trusted him, although he did cut me in my first attempt to make his team. I cried. Sadly, he died of a heart attack during his coaching reign of the Laurentian Lions; however, his coaching philosophy lived on through future athletic programs. He was just one of those guys.

Chris did ultimately make the team, and the Laurentian Lions won a couple of championships while he was playing. He played fullback and defensive back, but he excelled as a punter. He remembers getting increasingly better...and that he set some punting records at Laurentian that stood for decades.

Baseball First, Then Football

Chris actually preferred baseball to football, but his hopes for a baseball career as a left-handed pitcher were cut short when he failed to make the cut in the professional tryouts he had with the Montreal Expos and the Pittsburgh Pirates. After that, baseball began to take a back seat, and football took over as the new focus:

> Sports, in general, helped me move forward in life as far as developing a sense of who I was and where my strengths and weaknesses were. Participating in sports gave me more confidence.

The Harber Brothers

Chris couldn't continue talking about his career in sports without mentioning his brother Robin. He and Robin are very close in age, so they ended up playing football together throughout high school and college. Robin was also a punter, but he was a better overall athlete than Chris and was able to extend his career into the CFL.

Chris and Robin looked a lot alike, and Chris claims that their voices were even more similar. This worked well for Chris when his self-confidence got in the way of him asking a girl out on a date:

> We sounded identical. When there was a girl I wanted to date, and I was terrified to call her up, I'd get Robin to phone her. She'd think that she was talking to me, and Robin was cool as a cucumber because he had no investment in the relationship. We'd do things like that. We were fairly close.

> Coming out of their university playing days, Robin received a call from Coach Jack Gotta of the Ottawa Rough Riders asking him to come for a tryout. On the day of the tryout, Robin was not feeling well, so he asked Chris to take his place. Chris will never forget the look of disappointment on Jack Gotta's face when he timed him in

the 40-yard dash. He looked at him and said, 'Robin, do you have an injury or something?'

Robin went on to play for several years in the CFL. He played for the Calgary Stampeders and finished his career with Ottawa.

Best Years

Chris feels that his best years were when he was playing in high school. It meant so much to him that in 1982, on the 25th anniversary of the opening of Laurentian High School, he and Robin initiated and helped organize an alumni football game:

> It was a full contact game between football players from the 1960s and those from the 1970s. We played the game at R.D. Campbell Stadium, the same field where we'd played our home games when we were in high school. The participating players spent months getting into shape before the game. We even wore our old uniforms from when we played. We packed the stadium with old high school football fans. It was a huge success—like reliving a moment. That shows you how much I valued my high school football playing days. I enjoyed that time the most.

Playing for the Carleton Ravens

Chris says he chose Carleton U. in Ottawa to study Geology. His first year at Carleton, he did not play football. He did go out for the team during his second year, and he made the team but wasn't able to play because he'd been put on academic probation. Not being able to play motivated Chris to "buckle down" in the classroom so that he could get his eligibility back:

> One of my strengths is that I can do what it takes to get it done, whether it is on the football field or in the classroom, and I don't necessarily have to like it.

After completing his degree in Geology at Carleton, Chris decided to do post-graduate work at Queens University and pursue his teaching certificate. He also decided to play football for the Golden Gaels. He made the team, but his heart wasn't in football anymore, and he didn't finish the season.

Life After Football

One thing I have learned as I go through my journey in life is you do your best and move on. Be happy with that...easier said than done.

Prior to retirement, Chris spent his entire career working in federal public service, primarily involved in programs requiring water management:

> I spent my early years managing national ferry service subsidies. The federal government used to subsidize all the ferries across Canada, including BC, off the coast of Labrador, Prince Edward Island, etc. They ultimately divested the whole program over to the provinces. Later, I went on to work for Small Craft Harbours of Transport Canada, which included developing shoreline facilities for recreational boating and constructing breakwaters and marinas.
>
> I spent the last 15 years of my career working for the Canadian Coast Guard, where I managed a training program for new recruits. This job included developing computer-based training modules and distance learning techniques for adult learning.

Chris attributes football, and sports in general, as helping him in life. He reflected on how football introduced him to some key role models who kept him out of trouble and got him through some difficult times.

With regard to being selected to the All Canada Football Team, Chris said that while he felt fortunate to be chosen, it was still an honor.

Dave Kates #22

University of Alberta – Defensive Back
First Team All-Canadian – 1971 and 1972

His passion for sports, teaching, coaching, and his zest for life has been and will always be a part of his legacy. An exceptional athlete, Dave was always the model for bringing out the best in his teammates.
— *Larry Dufresne*

Dave grew up in Edmonton and attended Ross Sheppard High School. He played football and ran track for the T-Birds. His specialty was the 100-yard dash; in fact, he came in first in the 100-yard dash in the City of Edmonton track meet.

As was the case with most football players in Western Canada during this era, Dave was not recruited to play football. He took the obvious route and chose to enroll at the hometown University of Alberta and played football for the Golden Bears after playing one year of junior football for the Edmonton Huskies.

Dave's coaches at the University of Alberta described him as "determined, intense, and fast." He had great range on the field.

His teammate, Bob Keating, described Dave as "a team guy and a great leader."

Jim Donlevy, Dave's head coach at the University of Alberta, said:

> Dave was a detail guy. He spent hours in the film room studying upcoming opponents. His speed combined with his knowledge of his opponent's tendencies gave him a tremendous advantage on the field.

Dan McCaffery, another one of Dave's teammates at the University of Alberta, described him this way:

Dave was a wonderful person, a friend, and a great teammate. Words such as kind, witty, spirited, and, of course, talented, all fall just short of describing him.

Dave was drafted by the Edmonton Eskimos after the 1971 season and was their last cut coming out of training camp in 1972. He returned to the Golden Bears and was the captain of their Vanier Cup champion team in 1972.

Jim Donlevy recalls that Dave did not play in the Vanier Cup game against the Waterloo Lutheran Golden Hawks as he had been injured in the playoff game leading up to the Vanier Cup. Being captain of the team, Dave did participate in the kickoff ceremonies, and he gave up the opportunity to wear his uniform during the game to allow another player a chance to participate. The CIS had strict rules about how many players could suit up for each game, which was unfortunate because it kept members of the team who had contributed during the year from participating in the game.

After Football

After graduation, Dave became a teacher in the Edmonton School District. He worked for several years at McNally and Victoria Composite High Schools. Errol Johnson, one of his fellow teachers, had this to say about him:

> I worked with Dave at McNally. There was never a classier and more thoughtful person in our math department.

Final Thoughts

Rob McKenzie, another one of Dave's teammates, summed up the man that Dave was with these words:

> Dave was our heart and soul. I am so very blessed to be the person I have become for having known Dave.

The End Zone

Revelations

Bob Eccles felt that it might be interesting for me to share what I learned in this journey across Canada and time. I must say, I learned a lot about Canadian university football that I had never known.

Probably, the most surprising thing I learned had to do with the differences between the governance of football in Canada as compared to it in the U.S. As I mentioned previously, the fact that players in Canada could play for five years and for multiple schools came as a surprise. Eleven of the 24 players played football for more than one school. Also, a player in Canada could be drafted by a CFL team, but if he was cut before the regular season started, he could return to play more university football, assuming he hadn't played for the maximum of five years. In addition, even though the coaching staff at McMaster was made up primarily of former CFL players, I had not realized that this was true of most Canadian university football programs. Coaches in the U.S. are almost all former college football players, but few of them are former pro football players.

I also discovered that most Canadian university football programs in the late 60s and early 70s were lucky if they had a full-time coach, and it was rare for them to have more than one salaried coach on staff. The coaches' salaries, in most cases, were lower than what high school coaches were paid in the U.S.

Facts and Figures – Pro Football

While researching these 24 players, some interesting numbers surfaced.

○ Seventeen members of the 1971 team were drafted by the CFL and attended at least one CFL training camp. Of the seven who

did not attend camp, Denny Hrycaiko was drafted and offered a contract but decided to accept a scholarship to attend graduate school. Bob Mincarelli was considered an import and attended a New York Giants camp as a free agent. The remaining five were either too banged up after their university days or considered too small for professional football.
- Contracts offered to those drafted by the CFL ranged from $3,500 to $10,000. A number of players walked out of camp when they realized their playing time would be limited and that they could make more money teaching or pursuing a career in business.
- Three of the players, Wayne Conrad, Brian Gervais, and Larry Smith, played in the CFL for at least five years. Dan Dulmage played for two years then quit to begin his career as a dentist.

Multi-Year Selections

Of the 24 men who were honored with a selection to the All Canada team in 1971, it was the first and only selection for 14 of us. Seven were honored twice: John Buda, Dan Dulmage, Dave Kates, Paul Kilger, Bob Mincarelli, Larry Smith, and Mel Smith. Three players were selected to three All Canada teams: Max Abraham, Bob Eccles, and Jeannot Rodrigue.

Interesting Facts

When you look at this group of 24 men, there are some interesting facts that should be noted:

- Eighteen of the players coached at some point in their career. Four coached at the university level, including Denny Hrycaiko and Cam Innes, who became head coaches. Wayne Conrad coached for a while at the University of Calgary until the head coach realized he was beating the players up more than he was coaching them. Gill Bramwell became one of the most successful high school coaches in the history of football in Manitoba.
- All 24 members of the team played more than one sport.
- Many members of the team had scholarship opportunities to play hockey or football in the U.S.
- Two players, Paul Kilger and Jeannot Rodrigue, participated in fall training camps at U.S. universities. Both were turned off by

the lack of respect shown by the U.S. coaches toward their players and returned to Canada. Both ended up in Ottawa Gee-Gees uniforms.
○ Several players received scholarship offers to play for Simon Fraser University.
○ Eleven of us put on uniforms for more than one university

Vanier Cup Championships

Gill Bramwell, Ole Hensrud, and Denny Hrycaiko played on two Vanier Cup championship teams.

Dan Dulmage, George Hill, and Bruce MacRae played on the University of Western Ontario Vanier Cup championship team in 1971.

Cam Innes, Dave Kates, and Paul Kilger each played for a Vanier Cup championship team, and Cam Innes lead the Ottawa Gee-Gees into the Vanier Cup as their head coach in 1980.

I watched the Vanier Cup in 1971 from the stands and was on the field photographing the Vanier Cup in Vancouver in 2011 when McMaster defeated Laval 41–28 in double overtime.

Careers

Fifteen of the 24 members of the team pursued careers in business; eight pursued careers in education.

Dan Dulmage became a dentist.

The Apple Doesn't Fall Far From the Tree

Not surprisingly, several of the 1971 All Canada Team players have children who followed in their fathers' footsteps and experienced considerable success in sports. These included Brad Smith, Larry Smith's son, who was selected first team All Canadian at Queens and also played in the CFL. Max Abraham's sons, David and Brady, both played football for the Saskatoon Hilltops. Bob Eccles's daughter, Gina, was on the Canadian Olympic Weight Lifting team, and his son

Robbie played football and hockey and was once rated third in the world in Bike Polo.

Max Abraham wanted to make sure that I knew that his life long friend and teammate, Barrie Reid, has a son, Ryan, who was the quarterback for the University of Saskatchewan Huskies when they won the Vanier Cup in 1998. Ryan also became the first Huskie football player to play professional football in the United States.

If We Had a Chance to Do It Again

When asked if they would play football again, knowing what they know now, their answers depended upon the length of time they played and the toll the game took on their bodies. Two said they would probably not have played, and one took a long time to answer before saying that he would do it all again.

Before I started to write this book, I had a faint idea how to spell the word camaraderie. Now, I think it is the most used word in this book, and I will probably never misspell it again.

Fifteen of us will be meeting in Hamilton in late November 2017 to join in the Vanier Cup celebrations…and a reunion, of sorts.

www.ingramcontent.com/pod-product-compliance
Lightning Source LLC
Chambersburg PA
CBHW072344100426
42738CB00049B/1789